Reds, Rebels and Radicals

Reds, Rebels and Radicals

Derbyshire, Leicestershire and Nottinghamshire

David Bell

Five Leaves Publications

Reds, Rebels and Radicals
Derbyshire, Leicestershire and Nottinghamshire
David Bell

Published in 2019 by Five Leaves Publications
14a Long Row, Nottingham NG1 2DH
www.fiveleaves.co.uk
www.fiveleavesbookshop.co.uk

ISBN: 978-1-910170-63-2

Printed in Great Britain

Contents

Introduction 7

1. Len Wincott: Invergordon mutineer 9

2. Daniel Holt: campaigning newspaper owner and editor 15

3. Alice Hawkins: Leicester suffragette 21

4. The Amazing Kanes: a family of class warriors 27

5. Elizabeth Hooton: pioneer Quaker 31

6. George Powe: "a true comrade" 37

7. Alice Wheeldon: framed for conspiracy to murder 41

8. Elizabeth Heyrick: an "immediate" anti-slavery abolitionist 49

9. Bas Barker: a Chesterfield legend 53

10. Geoffrey Trease: Bows Against the Barons 59

11. Avtar Sadiq: Poet and IWA activist 67

12. Hannah Mitchell: a radical career based on two weeks' schooling 71

13. Ida Hackett: "a lady of quality, a life-long socialist" 77

14. Dennis Skinner: miner and socialist MP 83

15. A Cathedral of Unbelief and a Socialist Church 89

16. Walter Gregory: volunteer with the International Brigades 93

17. Malcolm Pinnegar and the Dirty Thirty 103

18. Jeremiah Brandreth and the Pentrich rising 109

Bibliography 119

Acknowledgements

I would like to thank the following people for their help in writing this book: Barry Johnson, Hilary Cave, Nick Hiles, Graham Stevenson, Jill Westby, Harsev Bains, Dyal Bagri, Alan Dorling, Ned Newitt, Malcolm Elliott, Kathy Bell, Miriam Gill, Deidre and Chloë Mason, Susan Knight, Ashton Civic Society, Paul Liversuch, Alan Warren, Peter Flack, Neil Bell, Chris Smith, Mandy Graham, Ruth Frudd, Jon Harris.

Introduction

The men and women featured in this book are an eclectic lot. There is a mutineer; a couple of suffragettes, one of them framed for conspiracy to murder the Prime Minister; a man who led a rebellion in 1817; an early Quaker who incurred the bigotry and wrath of the governor of Massachusetts; a volunteer with the International Brigades in the Spanish Civil War; a woman who fought for the abolition of slavery — taking on not only the slave-owners but also the gradualist approach advocated by William Wilberforce; the founder of the first newspaper in Newark, sent to prison for selling a Tom Paine pamphlet; an activist of the Windrush generation; and many others.

What they all have in common is that they had the courage and confidence to take on the power of the establishment: moral courage and often physical courage.

They are all heroes worth celebrating, women and men whose example can teach us about the importance of being willing to stand up and fight against cruelty, against unfairness, against bigotry. They show us what it means to be a rebel and a radical.

1. Len Wincott: Invergordon mutineer

Len Wincott was born in Dorset Street, Leicester, in 1907. He was one of eight children of an alcoholic father, a bricklayer, who terrorised his family. Len described his father as an illiterate drunken bully, a bricklayers' Ivan the Terrible, who thrashed his children with a well-oiled strap that hung from a nail next to his fireside rocking chair. He also used his fists on his family, and if his wife intervened — Len described her as a strong bulwark between the "booze-angered deity" and the children — she bore the brunt of the blows. Len's mother was as firm as a rock. She also delivered many of the local children, and she was the one who shamed many a young local lad into marrying his pregnant girlfriend.

When Len was four he was enrolled at Catherine Street Elementary School, where again he was beaten if he made any mistakes in his schoolwork. When he was a little older, he was often caned by the music teacher for singing out of tune. Len was not allowed to explain that he spent his evenings selling the *Leicester Mercury* round the local streets, bawling out his wares, ruining his vocal cords.

Several important events in Len's life occurred in 1919. When he was twelve, the school ran a mock election. The popular captain of the school was selected as the Conservative candidate, and Len volunteered to be the Labour candidate, despite — or perhaps because of — the fact that his own father was a loud and vocal Tory. The two candidates had to make a speech to the class, and to everyone's amazement Len wiped the floor with his opponent, answering all the questions put to him with ease. The headmaster, who had heard Len's speech through the open classroom door, was so impressed that he gave Len a diploma that would enable him to attend night-school classes. Len's pride was demolished when he took it home and his father threw it into the fire.

Not long after that, Len organised his first strike. An aeroplane had made a forced landing on a nearby field and the boys all hoped that the headmaster would give them the afternoon off to go and see it. This did not happen, so at noon Len spread the news that instead of going home, the children should gather for a protest meeting on a piece of wasteland next to the school. Len was picked as the speaker, and amid loud cheers, called for a strike. They all set off to march to the field where the plane had landed, but were overtaken by teachers on bicycles who were waving canes! The children were rounded up and herded back to school. The headmaster — cane in hand — demanded the name of the ringleader. Before Len could speak, another boy stood up and announced that there was no ringleader; they were all of one mind. They were all caned, but I cannot help seeing the boy who had spoken up as an embryonic "I am Spartacus" figure.

It was also in 1919 that Len lied about his age — claiming that he was fourteen — and fulfilled every schoolboy's dream of joining a circus. The circus was in Leicester and Len got a job there, fully intending to leave town when it moved on. However, his dream was shattered. Appalled by the cruelty to animals he witnessed — he saw a shackled bear, its maw clasped in a metal muzzle, being slashed about the head with a whip — he left the circus and returned home. Although a hero to his schoolmates for joining a circus, Len was thrashed by his teachers for this adventure.

Len left school at the age of thirteen, and got a job as a tea-boy/errand boy in a hosiery factory. Three years later he followed up his earlier attempt to run away with the circus with a successful decision to run away to sea. He joined the Royal Navy and sailed on HMS Norfolk to the Far East where he helped fight pirates in the China Sea. Len enjoyed his life as a sailor. At last he was receiving a real education, although he was informed that no matter how many exams he passed, he would always be a member of the lower ranks. At that time, there was no promotion from the ranks to the officer class. An officer was born an officer.

By 1931, the country was in financial difficulties brought about by the Great Depression. The Prime Minister, Ramsay MacDonald, had deserted his own Labour Party and formed a National Government with members of the Conservatives. The Government ordered drastic cuts, including lowering the pay of soldiers and sailors in the armed services. The Navy was to bear the greatest cuts. Officers were to have their pay cut by 3% but the ratings, the ordinary sailors, were to have their already inadequate pay and pensions slashed by 25%.

The Atlantic fleet was anchored off the Scottish coast. There had been no rumblings of dissatisfaction from the lower decks until this point. Virtually all the ratings were content with their conditions. They had no dispute with their immediate officers, no complaints of ill treatment. They all thought that the Navy was a place where a man could make something of himself. But when they read the notice put up on the morning of Sunday 13th September, there was a spontaneous reaction of disbelief and horror at what the Admiralty had decreed. The whole fleet was angry and ready for action, and it was Len Wincott who made the first move.

He knew his own shipmates on HMS Norfolk were with him, but how could they spread the word to the other six ships? There was a Church of England service held on each individual ship, but those sailors who were Roman Catholics attended a service held on a different ship each Sunday. This meant that all the Catholic sailors had to go to the ship where the service was held. Len asked the Catholic sailors to check the feelings on the other ships when they attended this service, and told them to announce that a meeting would be held that afternoon on shore.

At 2pm, Len entered the shore canteen, a WWI wooden structure overlooking four football pitches. As he entered, he saw that all the tables bar one were occupied. The atmosphere was extraordinarily quiet; there was no shouting or swearing. The men were sober and attentive. Len stood on the one remaining table and spoke to the men, who seemed to be waiting for a lead. "We must strike," he said, "like the miners." In a very short speech, he went on to speak of the poverty and degradation that the men — and more importantly their families — would face if the cuts went through. There was no clapping or cheering, but when he asked for a representative from each ship to come forward and say a few words, there was a rush of men to support his call. This was the turning point. Len knew that any man who came forward would be putting himself in a precarious position. Had the men been reluctant to put themselves on the line in this way, the action would have fizzled out. But the men were united in their determination. Their solidarity was impressive.

Shore leave was only until 8pm, so all the men returned to their own ships by that time. Rumours about the meeting had begun to reach the officers. There had been an informant — known in Navy circles as a "white rat" — who had attended the meeting and taken the news back to the wardroom. Fortunately, no one had identified Len Wincott as the first speaker at the meeting. He had taken the precaution of carrying his cap with the name of his ship hidden. Also, he had not been wearing his normal jumper with his good conduct badge on the left arm and his gunner's badge on the right arm. The white rat had not been able to identify him, and those who knew Len were not saying anything.

The following day, a second meeting was held on shore, and it was decided that the strike should begin the next morning, Tuesday 15th, at 6am. This meeting was interrupted by a Naval officer who demanded that the meeting should stop. When no one obeyed him, he realised that his patrol members had been surrounded by the ratings near the door. He was on his own in the middle of the room, and when someone dropped a glass which shattered loudly, he threw himself to the ground, then performed a rapid strategic withdrawal. The men returned to their ships in orderly fashion.

The following morning, the men of HMS Norfolk refused to take the ship out on exercises. As the captain addressed the men on the quarter deck, the ratings all left and went to the forecastle. The Marines had also agreed to throw in their lot with the men. The same was happening on the other six ships: the whole fleet was united in the refusal of duty. As each crew refused to obey the order, a cheer went up that could be heard by the men on the other ships.

In Civvy Street, this would be regarded as a strike — industrial action — but this was the Royal Navy and therefore it was Mutiny.

Len Wincott was the main author of a statement of protest drawn up by the mutineers, which said that the men were not complaining about the principle of cuts, but they were against the fact that the lower ranks would be the hardest hit.

The Admiralty were aghast at the sensational news that the men of the Navy were in revolt, especially when they found that the Marines — normally the force used to put down indiscipline in the ranks — were backing the sailors. Sir Austin Chamberlain, the First Lord of the Admiralty, promised the men that their demands would be considered, and he also promised that there would be "no victimisation". The Admiralty did halve the pay cuts, but it did not keep its promise that the men would not be victimised. Len Wincott was dismissed, along with a further 120 men who had taken part in what became known all over the world as the Invergordon Mutiny.

By now Len had become a working class hero to thousands, and he soon became a popular speaker at meetings all over the country. Some of these meetings were organised by the Communist Party, and eventually Len joined the Party. This suited the government and their supporters in the press. They could now say that the Invergordon Mutiny was a red plot, organised by communists. Privately, it was conceded that this was untrue: the mutiny was an instantaneous reaction to the unfairness of the pay cuts. In Leonard Wincott's later MI5 file, it states that MI5 now accepts that the mutiny was spontaneous and not communist-inspired, though it notes that this view was not generally accepted at the time.

A year later Len emigrated to live in Russia. Initially he worked in a factory, but he also did some language teaching. He became a Soviet citizen and when war broke out, he became a soldier in the Russian army. He endured the horrors of the siege of Leningrad, which lasted 900 days and cost a million lives.

A year after the war ended, Red Len, the workers' hero, was accused of "agitation against the Soviet State." As the Cold War developed, Joseph Stalin was seeing Western spies everywhere, and the fact that Len Wincott had once been a member of the British Royal Navy was enough to make him a suspect. He was found guilty and sent to work in a coal mine in Siberia.

When Stalin died in 1953, his successor, Nikita Khrushchev, had many prisoners released from the gulags. Len was released, and returned to life in Moscow. His wife Anna had died during his ten years in the gulag, and he now married Olga, a woman he had met in the labour camp. By now, Len could speak eight languages and both he and Olga worked as translators. They divorced in 1965, and Len married Lena Vasilyena whom he had met at the Foreign Languages Institute in Moscow. Lena was his third and final Russian wife. However, while Len was touring England in the 1930s as a speaker after the Mutiny, he had met and married an American girl. As there is no record of a divorce from this first wife, it may be that his subsequent three marriages in Russia were actually bigamous.

Invergordon mutineer, Russian soldier, a prisoner in Stalin's gulags — Len's life had already more packed into it than most. But even after he retired, Len's fascinating story was not over. In his 60s, Len's life took on a new aspect. He became a film star, and appeared in many Russian films, ironically playing the roles of foreign spies or English aristocrats.

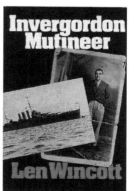

In 1974, he wrote his autobiography *Invergordon Mutineer*, and was allowed to visit England to publicise his book. He was not allowed to stay, and spent the last years of his life in Moscow. When Red Len died in January 1983, his ashes were returned to England and scattered off the English coast, in the presence of his widow Lena, and George Hill, an old shipmate from his days at Invergordon.

2. Daniel Holt: campaigning newspaper owner and editor

Elections in the 1790s were corrupt and extremely undemocratic. Indeed even the use of the word "democracy" indicated that the speaker was a dangerous revolutionary, guilty of sedition and probably treason.

In county constituencies voting was restricted to men — never women — who owned freehold land worth forty shillings a year. If you didn't own property, you had no vote. Voting in boroughs was more varied. Industrial cities like Sheffield and Manchester had no MPs at all, while some constituencies of a few dozen houses would elect two. Often elections were not contested. The local landowner would put forward his candidate and he became the Member of Parliament for the area. Where there was another candidate, voters were usually given a payment — the common bribe was usually two guineas — to buy their vote. And if you were a tenant of the local landowner, you were expected to vote for his candidate.

In a few boroughs, there was a "scot and lot" system, where any man who paid a local tax (a scot) could vote. The scot was to pay for the local poorhouse, and the word "scot" lives on in the phrase "scot-free".

One man who did oppose the corruption and advocated a radical stance was Thomas Paine. Paine emigrated to the British American colonies in 1774 in time to participate in the American revolution. He wrote the pamphlet *Common Sense*, which advocated America's independence from Britain. General George Washington even ordered his officers to read out Paine's work to their men before battle, and many believe that Tom Paine helped his friend Thomas Jefferson write the American Declaration of Independence.

America disowned Paine after the later publication of *The Age of Reason*, which argued against organized religion. They were also alarmed to discover that Tom Paine believed that the rights of man should apply to all — including slaves, Native Americans and women.

Paine went to France in 1790 and became involved in the French Revolution. He was elected to the French National Convention — the revolutionary parliament — though he made an enemy of Robespierre. In 1791 he wrote *The Rights of Man*, defending the French Revolution against its critics. Because of this, the British government had him tried in his absence for seditious libel. However, because he could not be imprisoned — he was not living in Britain

— the government decided they would punish anyone who supported his ideals.

One such man was Daniel Holt, a printer from Newark, in Nottinghamshire. Newark resident Dr Alan Dorling tells me that he is pleased that Daniel Holt is included in this book of East Midlands' radicals, since "both the town and the county have written him out of history." That Newark should have chosen to expunge this local man, Daniel Holt, from its story is remarkable, since Holt played such an important part in it. Alan has written articles about Newark at the time of Holt, and I am grateful for his permission to use material from two pieces "A Friend of Liberty" and "Loyalism in Newark," published in *The Nottingham Historian*.

Daniel Holt was born in 1766 in Newark, then a town of around 6,500 people. His father Simeon was a seedsman, but Daniel did not join him in this trade. Instead he became an apprentice at Allin and Co., a Newark printer. He soon made friends with Joseph Gales, who was an apprentice at another Newark firm of printers, Tomlinson's, and the two young men found they shared an interest in radical politics.

Joe Gales went on to found and edit the *Sheffield Register*, a radical newspaper. Daniel Holt stayed in Newark, and campaigned for democratic reform there.

Newark had the scot and lot system, so the town had far more men able to vote than in the rest of the country, but it also meant that that politics in the town was always a rough trade — a hard-fought affair. In the 1790 parliamentary election at Newark, the Duke of Newcastle evicted some three dozen of his tenants for voting for the Whig candidate, rather than his own Tory candidate. Voting then was definitely not secret, and, as a tenant, you were expected to support the candidate your aristocratic landlord put forward.

Although Daniel Holt was a courageous and doughty radical, it would be a mistake to call him a Red. In the Newark politics of the late eighteenth century, they wore their colours the other way round. The Red faction supported the establishment and the Blues fought for reform! The Reds were followers of the Duke of Newcastle and the Duke of Rutland, both high Tory local aristocrats, and they supported the government of William Pitt and the monarchy of George III. Thus the Reds were Tories and the Blues were dissenters — all very confusing to the modern reader — though in the USA blue equals Democrats and Republicans are red!

The Blue faction was more progressive, and ranged all the way from the Duke of Portland, a rather conservative Whig politician, to those who were advocates of much more radical reform. This wing of the Blue faction — mainly artisans and shopkeepers, many of them dissenters — supported the aims of the revolutions in France and America. They would discuss the works of Tom Paine — *Common Sense* and *The Rights of Man* — and argue about his republican ideals. Tom Paine was a great hero to these reformers. He was — and still is — a charismatic figure for all radicals, so it is hardly surprising that Daniel Holt was a great admirer of Paine and his work.

When Daniel completed his printing apprenticeship, he married his childhood sweetheart Eliza Hankin, and set up as a printer in his own right. Originally based at a shop in Bridge Street, he then moved to Stodman Street. Among his early publications was a history of Newark. He also established the *Newark Herald*, the town's first newspaper. Like other newspapers, it carried reports of local news, agricultural prices and job vacancies, but the *Herald* also campaigned for the abolition of the slave trade, for public and constitutional reform, and supported the French revolutionaries. And when you bought your copy of the *Newark Herald*, there would often be a free radical pamphlet tucked inside.

Not everyone in Newark supported the reformist arguments put forward in the *Herald*. The government was fearful of a French-style revolution coming to Britain and saw any calls for reform, however reasonable, as seditious. In 1792, they issued a Royal Proclamation against seditious publications, and throughout the country local loyalist associations — known as Crown and Anchor Associations — for "Preserving Liberty and Property against Republicans and Levellers" were established. "Preserving Property" was the prime task of the loyalist associations; "Preserving Liberty" certainly did not apply to the liberty of people like Tom Paine and Daniel Holt.

The Newark Loyalist Association issued a statement that "there are many factious and disorderly persons who by their seditious publications and criminal conversations are endeavouring to subvert the constitution of this country and to ferment anarchy and confusion." The reference to "criminal conversations" reveals how the Loyalist Associations were opposed to all ideas of free speech that did not conform to their own opinions: all conversations ought to meet with their loyalist — and partisan — approval. The reference to "seditious publications" meant that trouble was brewing for the Newark radical printer Daniel Holt.

The Newark Loyalist Association included many local people of wealth and influence. At its first meeting there were aldermen, clergymen, business leaders and lawyers. The mayor was present, along with sixteen past or future mayors. At their second meeting, they appointed a man to "expunge from the walls of Newark any seditious writings or expressions leading to disaffection to the King or Constitution." In other words, only posters supporting their own faction would be allowed. The Association's most important preoccupation was to silence the *Newark Herald* and Daniel Holt.

The town clerk, Job Brough, had once taken Daniel to court, alleging that he had been libelled. In a far from unbiased court, Daniel was found guilty and sentenced to six months, but while he was in prison and after his release, the *Herald* continued to thrive. Perhaps people were buying the paper to show that they thought the attacks on him were unfair and politically motivated.

The Newark establishment had always hated the leaders of the reform community. One early hate figure was the moderate William Dickinson, a small landowner and a magistrate, a leading supporter of the conservative Whig, the Duke of Portland. But now the bête noir of the Newark Loyalist Association became Daniel Holt. One relatively minor irritation that seemed to annoy the loyalists was that one of Daniel's employees took to wearing a cap with the words LIBERTY AND EQUALITY on it. Very French! Very un-English. They were outraged and determined to have their revenge.

A clergyman member of the loyalist faction went into Daniel's shop and bought two pamphlets, both of which Daniel was happy to sell to him. One was an article written ten years earlier by Major John Cartwright, entitled *Address to the Tradespeople, Mechanics, Labourers and other Inhabitants of the town of Newark, on a Parliamentary Reform.* The second pamphlet was by Tom Paine, and was his response to the Royal Proclamation issued by the government. It opposed not only the government itself, but also those reformers who believed that Parliament might reform itself voluntarily.

The Newark loyalists sent the two tracts to the Attorney General, and in 1793 Daniel Holt was charged with having printed the Cartwright pamphlet and having sold the Paine one. In February of that year, war between France and Britain was declared. This made things much worse for those reformers who had always publicly supported the French Revolution. They could now be said to be not only seditious, but also treasonous.

At this time, Holt was also publishing another series of pamphlets entitled *The Briton*. This was a moderate publication which attempted to argue that reform should be gradual and "from within". It had no time for Tom Paine, and Daniel published it as a contribution to public debate, while not agreeing with its sentiments himself. Even this mildly reformist periodical outraged the loyalists, for whom the British Constitution could not be reformed as it was already ideal. Perfection could not be improved!

Daniel's trial took place in July 1793. He was represented by the renowned Whig lawyer, Thomas Erskine, who pointed out that Holt was not the original publisher of the *Address*, but had simply reprinted it at the request of the Nottingham Political Society. Secondly, he had not actively advertised or promoted the Paine pamphlet, but had only sold it to people coming in and asking for it. But the carefully selected jury found Daniel Holt guilty.

The verdict had a startling effect in Newark. The walls of the town were soon covered in painted messages calling for all Englishmen to rise up and fight for Liberty. The people of Newark had obviously decided that if the reformist message could not be printed legally, then the only possible route was through revolt and through slogans painted on the walls by night.

In November, Holt returned to the court for sentencing. Most people in Newark, including many who were not reformers, thought that he would perhaps be given a fine, or at worst a short sentence. However, the government and the local hard-line loyalists were determined to make an example of him, and he was given a four year prison sentence, on top of a £100 fine.

Daniel Holt did not go quietly. Before he was hauled off to Newgate Prison, he pointed out in the pages of the *Newark Herald* that his only crime was to call for universal liberty, and to be opposed to an unpopular war and to a corrupt government.

Once in Newgate, Daniel found himself in good company, sharing a room with two London booksellers who had sold reformist periodicals — including the *Herald*. He found that the prison was full of radicals imprisoned for alleged sedition and treason. More men were jailed for these crimes in the seven year period from 1792 to 1799 than in the whole of the previous century. It had become the favourite means of the Pitt administration for dealing with anyone calling for parliamentary reform.

Daniel continued to campaign from his prison cell. His book *A Vindication of the Conduct and Principles of the Printer of the Newark Herald* was written in prison, and published in 1794. In it, he called on the people of Newark to consider what had happened to him. He fiercely lambasted those in his home town who had attempted to blacken his character, misrepresent his principles and destroy his domestic happiness.

The *Vindication* was popular enough to run to a second edition, but it was a final clarion call from the Newark radical. During his incarceration, first *The Briton* and then the *Newark Herald* ceased publication. The loyalists in Newark had succeeded in silencing the voice of reform. The reformist Blue faction split, with conservative Whigs — including the Duke of Portland — joining the Pitt government in a coalition. Out in the countryside, loyalist mobs rioted against all reformists, with Paine frequently burnt in effigy. In Newark, the effigy may have been thought to symbolise Daniel Holt too.

Daniel Holt was released from prison in 1797, having served his full four-year term. His health was shattered and he died two years later at the age of thirty-three.

So was his life and work entirely in vain? Maybe not. Holt's widow Eliza remarried and with her new husband, Matthew Hage, carried on Daniel's work with their own printing firm, which continued to campaign for parliamentary reform.

Although for some decades elections in Newark were uncontested — the Tory candidate was returned unopposed — eventually in 1832, a reformist candidate was finally elected to Parliament for the Newark constituency. It took a long while to arrive, but eventually many of the reforms advocated by Daniel Holt did come into being. A vindication indeed.

3. Alice Hawkins: Leicester suffragette

Alice Hawkins was born on 4th March 1863, one of nine children of Henry Shaw, a travelling journeyman-shoemaker. At some time during her early childhood her family settled in Leicester. Alice left school at the age of thirteen to work in the boot and shoe trade, initially as a fitter who helped tighten the leather for the more skilled workers. She soon became aware that the women in the factory were paid far less than their male colleagues, and their working conditions were worse too.

In her early twenties Alice found work at the Equity shoe factory then situated on Friar's Causeway, a newly-founded workers' co-operative. The workers there were encouraged to join NUBSO, the National Union of Boot and Shoe Operatives, and to take part in political activity. In 1884 she married Alfred Hawkins, an active socialist, and together they had seven children. Family life did not tie Alice down. In 1892 she joined the Independent Labour Party and three years later she formed and helped to run the ILP women's auxiliary organisation. The following year a Women's Co-operative Guild was started at the Equity shoe factory, and Alice was once again one of its leading members. She was elected as a NUBSO representative to Leicester Trades Council, and in 1905 she was involved in organising an unemployment march to London.

By this time Alice was becoming somewhat disillusioned and disappointed with the Trade Union movement as a vehicle for improving the position of women. They seemed more interested in their men, seen as the main breadwinner of the family.

Alice had met members of the Pankhurst family in the 1890s, and again in 1905 when Christabel came to speak to the Leicester Trades Council, but it was February 1907 before she attended a meeting of their Women's Social and Political Union in London. Following the meeting in Hyde Park, the WSPU activists marched to the House of Commons to demand votes for women. Mounted police attacked the march, and Alice was one of the women arrested. She was charged with obstructing the police and sentenced to fourteen days in Holloway Prison. This was her first taste of prison, but not her last.

The spell in prison did nothing to daunt the spirit of Alice and her comrades, even though they were put in separate cells to prevent them from "conspiring". Supporters hired the London Excelsior Brass Band to play rousing WSPU music outside the prison, so that the women could hear it from their cells. They were released one by one at 9 am, presumably in the hope that they would creep away. The authorities couldn't have got it more wrong. As each prisoner was released, she was greeted by a cheering crowd of 200 supporters. They marched off into central London for a breakfast addressed by George Bernard Shaw, a leading supporter of their cause. At this breakfast, Alice read out a letter from her Leicester MP. Although he expressed his regrets that Alice had been arrested, he also said that he thought the actions of the women would put back their cause. The name of this rather "conservative" MP? Ramsay MacDonald. I can imagine that those women hearing his advice greeted it with loud disdain!

Alice returned to Leicester where, with the full support of her husband Alfred, she founded the Leicester Branch of WSPU. Sylvia Pankhurst spent some time in Leicester that year, and she later wrote, "At night I held meetings for the local WSPU, amongst whom only Mrs Hawkins as yet dared mount the platform." While Sylvia Pankhurst was

in Leicester she, not surprisingly, visited the Equity shoe factory. Sylvia was an artist and she drew a sketch in pastels of one of the Equity women workers. The picture is believed to be of Alice Hawkins, and in 2002, it was purchased at a Sotheby's auction for £9,400 by Leicester City Museum. It is not on permanent display — it would fade — but can be seen on request.

There is a blue plaque in honour of Alice Hawkins on the wall of the former Equity shoe factory in Western Road.

The Leicester branch of WSPU began to campaign in Leicester and Leicestershire, speaking in town squares, on village greens and at factory gates. They called for women's suffrage, and frequently complained that the trade unions were not doing enough for their female members. They also tried to attend political meetings. In 1909, Alice was refused entry to a Liberal Party meeting held at the Palace Theatre, so her husband went inside in her stead while Alice protested outside. Alfred Hawkins interrupted the speaker — Winston Churchill — and demanded to know why the government refused votes for women. When he asked how Churchill dared stand on a democratic platform, Alfred was forcibly ejected from the meeting. Together with Alice and other supporters, they besieged the doors, asking to be allowed back in. They were all arrested and as Alice refused to pay a fine, she was again sentenced to fourteen days, this time in Leicester Prison. On this occasion she took part in a prison hunger strike along with Helen Watts from the neighbouring county of Nottingham.

Alfred attempted to heckle Winston Churchill at another meeting, and he was attacked by violent stewards who threw him down a flight of steps. His leg was fractured and he sued the Liberal Party. He won his case and was awarded £100, a considerable sum in the first decade of the twentieth century. Peter Barratt, the great-grandson of Alfred and Alice Hawkins, tells me that there is a family story that Alfred purchased an off-licence in Leicester with the compensation money.

Not all the listeners to her speeches were sympathetic. On one occasion she was speaking in Leicester Marketplace when a heckler shouted that she should get off home to her family. She was able to smile and point to Alfred and her teenage children by her side. "Here they are," she said with understandable pride. "They are my supporters." The Leicester authorities tried to use this antipathy and violence from some elements of the crowd to dissuade Alice from addressing open-air meetings, but she refused to accept this. Her Leicester meetings attracted large numbers of people, both pro and anti, and had to be attended by a police presence. Alice was not just an activist in her home area. In 1908, she addressed a mass meeting of 250,000 supporters in Hyde Park, and in *The Times* of the next day she was described as a keynote speaker.

Unlike the Pankhurst family, Alice was definitely a working-class woman, living in a very ordinary area of Leicester. When she was needed for a meeting in London, the Pankhursts would send a car for her. Her neighbours must have been amazed when a huge chauffeur-driven car managed to crawl down the back streets of Leicester to pick up Alice.

Alice Hawkins served three further prison sentences for breaking windows — including one at the Home Office, for which she got twenty-

£100 DAMAGES
FOR
ILLEGAL EJECTION.

At Leeds Assizes, on the 23rd and 24th of March, 1911, before Mr. Justice Avory and a special jury, Mr. Alfred Hawkins was awarded £100 DAMAGES AND COSTS against the Committee of the Bradford League of Young Liberals, for his forcible ejection from a meeting at St. George's Hall, Bradford, addressed by the Right Hon. Winston Churchill, M.P. on November 26th, 1910.

WHAT TOOK PLACE.—"When Mr. Churchill was referring to the question about the House of Lords as being now reached in final stage, Mr. Hawkins stood up and said "What you say applies equally to the women who are demanding the vote." He was immediately seized by a number of stewards, run out of the hall and ejected down a staircase with such violence that his kneecap received a double fracture."

Mr. JUSTICE AVORY, summing up, said, " A mere Intervention, such as has been proved in this case, does not authorise either the Chairman of the meeting or the stewards or anybody else summarily to eject that person from the meeting without previous request to him to go. . . . Until he has been requested to leave and his licence to be there has been determined, any person who lays hands upon him and turns him out of that meeting and out of his seat, IS IN LAW COMMITTING AN ASSAULT."

LIBERALS! Remember these words of the Learned Judge and do not commit an assault when those who cherish Liberal PRINCIPLES ABOVE PARTY assert a Briton's right to Free Speech even IN THE PRESENCE OF A CABINET MINISTER.

Price 6d. per 100, 4/- per 1,000.
Mr. Justice Avory's Summing-up in full may be obtained Price 1d. each.

Printed by the Metropolitan Printing Works Company Limited, 14 Bartletts' Buildings, Holborn, London, E.C.

one days — and for pouring red ink into pillar boxes in Leicester's Granby Street. She frequently refused to eat while in prison. Suffragettes often used prison hunger strikes as part of their protests, and were force-fed so violently that they had their teeth broken.

Dissatisfied with the unsympathetic attitude of NUBSO, she formed a trade union for female workers in the boot and shoe factories — the

Independent National Union of Women Boot and Shoe Workers. Founded by Alice Hawkins and Lizzie Wilson in 1911, the union continued in existence until the 1930s. Alice lived in Leicester for the rest of her life, and died at the age of 83, a lifelong supporter of the trade union and Labour movement. On her death in March 1946, the *Leicester Mail* headline was: CITY SUFFRAGETTE DEAD: JAILED FIVE TIMES IN FIGHT FOR WOMEN'S VOTE. It is not surprising that she is one of Leicester's favourite daughters, a genuine Leicester hero.

Alice's granddaughter often told her son, Peter Barratt, "My grandmother said to me when I was a teenager, you must use your vote, we suffered for it, and I always have." Peter regards that as a lesson we should all heed. He is very proud of his descent from this feisty woman. "She was a determined and valiant woman," he told me, "who stood up for what she believed in." He is proud of his great-grandfather Alfred too, adding, "Throughout her time as a suffragette, Alice benefited greatly from the strong support of her husband and of her employer, Equity Shoes."

A 7ft bronze statue of Alice Hawkins, created by sculptor Sean Hedges-Quinn, was unveiled in Leicester's Market Square on 4th February 2018.

"Suffragette" was originally a term of contempt coined by the *Daily Mail* implying "the little girlies who want the vote" — but it was picked up and used by the more militant women. "Suffragist" was the term used by the less militant supporters — men or women — who campaigned for women's votes.

Another Leicester suffragette was machinist Ellen Sherriff. She too was in favour of direct action to achieve the vote. She slipped out of her home in the middle of the night of 12th July 1914, and with a colleague, Ellen set fire to Blaby's wooden railway station. Although it was known that suffragettes had caused the conflagration — they had left copies of their newspaper *The Suffragette* — the two culprits were never discovered. It was not until after Ellen's death that her nephew Harry Murby felt able to publicise his aunt's action. "The Leicester suffragettes were split into two groups, the peaceful ones and the militant ones," he said, "and Ellen was definitely a militant one."

Carole Claridge from Hinckley recalls her great-aunt Gracie Ball who began working for the cause of women's suffrage, chaining herself to railings at the age of sixteen. Unlike the family of Alice Hawkins, Gracie's family was shocked by her actions, especially when she was sent to prison. Gracie was disowned by her family, and died in poverty in the workhouse in 1928.

The fight of women like Alice Hawkins, Ellen Sherriff and Gracie Ball led to some women being given the vote in 1918. Discrimination still prevailed however, and it was only women over thirty were given the franchise, compared with men who could vote at twenty-one. It was not until 1928 that women achieved parity with male voters.

4. The Kanes: a family of class warriors

The Kane family arrived in Staveley, near Chesterfield, in 1929. They were originally miners from Fife, but had been blacklisted for being strong trade unionists. They first walked from Scotland to Durham, but even there they found their militant reputation had preceded them. There was no work for them in the Durham pits, and so they arrived in north Derbyshire.

Jock, Mick and Patrick got jobs in the local pits, and began organizing their workmates to form a miners' union to campaign for better wages. One of their early recruits was local man Tom Swain, who later became MP for North East Derbyshire. They began to duplicate and distribute a publication called *The Staveley Sparks*, which discussed the difficult conditions the miners worked in.

They were, however, living in three Staveley Company houses — tied cottages — so when the company decided to sack the Kane miners, they were evicted and put on the streets. When the bailiffs came to throw them out, Martin Kane — the patriarch of the family — was ill with TB, but he was unceremoniously carried out from his bed. He should have gone straight into hospital, but the powers-that-be decided that they were now homeless, and were therefore the responsibility of the Fife authorities, back where their roots were.

The Kane family turned to the relieving officer to ask for help for Martin, and he was eventually taken into the workhouse attached to Scarsdale Hospital. The rest of the family still needed somewhere to live. They tried to find individual lodgings, only to find that the Staveley Company had informed all its tenants that any family taking in a member of the Kane family would themselves be evicted. Mine owners were not known for their compassion.

One family — devout members of the Salvation Army — decided that this was cruel and un-Christian. This family showed compassion and a great deal of courage, and they took some of the Kane men as lodgers. The women — wives and sisters — and the older children had to go into the workhouse and the younger Kane children were sent to a children's home in Brampton. The children's home provided them with three decent meals a day, and they were allowed to see their parents each weekend.

All this trauma had been put into effect just to stop the Kane men recruiting local miners into the union. The scandal of what the coal owners had done to the family was obvious to everyone, and two months later, a landlord in Staveley let them have a large three-storey house on Chesterfield Road, where the whole family could live together.

Mick Kane, unable to find work at the Derbyshire mines, went to lodge with a family in Harworth, in Nottinghamshire. Eventually he found work at the local Harworth Colliery. There he helped to establish a branch of the Nottinghamshire Miners' Association — in competition with the right-wing "Spencer Union" that was already in existence.

After the 1926 miners' strike — which began as a seven-day general strike, but then became a protracted miners' strike — MP George Spencer had decided to form an anti-strike "union". Officially titled the Nottingham and District Miners' Industrial Union, it was commonly termed the Spencer Union. The mine owners were delighted and the Spencer "scab" Union became the only one the owners would recognise. The mine owners in Bolsover and Cresswell in neighbouring Derbyshire even declared their pits were now part of the Nottinghamshire coalfield and insisted on their miners being in the Spencer Union. Those readers who believe that history does repeat itself might see a close parallel with the formation of the Union of Democratic Mineworkers after the 1984–5 miners' strike!

Mick Kane and like-minded miners began to campaign for a real union at Harworth. In 1937, they forced the company to hold a ballot on the issue — which union did the men want to represent them? Despite the fact that an overwhelming majority voted for the Nottingham Miners' Association over the hated Spencer Union, the result was ignored by the company. Unbelievably — in view of the vote — the company repeated that would only recognise the Spencer Union.

This led to a massive dispute and the men at Harworth pit came out on strike. There was tremendous support in the mining villages, and a huge police presence was required in each village to allow the few blacklegs — those scabs who wanted to carry on working — to go into the mine. Two solid lines of policemen would line up in each village to form a narrow channel for the scabs to get through. Outside the police lines, the women would line up to "pan them in." They would bang saucepan lids, dustbin lids, and anything else they could rattle to provide an ironic musical accompaniment as the scabs scuttled past. They were, in the time-honoured way, preventing the blacklegs from creeping in quietly.

The police deliberately tried to provoke the strikers, and Mick Kane was arrested. He was actually trying to quell a disturbance, but was alleged to have been the leader of it. He was charged, found guilty and sent to prison for three years. However, it was due to this strike and the fight led by Mick Kane that national negotiations took place leading to an amalgamation of the Spencer Union with the Nottinghamshire Miners' Association to form the Nottinghamshire Miners' Federation as part of the Miners' Federation of Great Britain. This later became the National Union of Mineworkers (NUM).

After his release from prison, Mick Kane went to work at Grassmoor Colliery in Derbyshire, where he became a full-time union official.

Mick's brother Jock had played a big part in Chesterfield in the National Unemployed Workers Movement and in various anti-fascist organizations. He became a full-time organizer in Sheffield for the Communist Party, but returned to mining in South Yorkshire. He was so highly regarded among the mining community that, after nationalization in 1947, he became one of the labour officers — a sort of personnel manager. But being part of management was so much against his beliefs and his whole way of life that he resigned his post and went back as an ordinary miner. He continued to play a role within the NUM.

People who knew the Kane family tell me that it was not just the men of the family who were activists. The women were also towers of strength. Mary Kane, who became Mary MacMahon, was a lifelong Labour Party member, and became a leading councillor on Staveley Urban District Council. Kate went into service in London, married an Italian and ran a transport café. Bridget, who never married, became the matriarch of the Kane family, bringing up her nephews and nieces and providing a home for any member of the family who needed it.

The Kanes were an amazing family of activists.

5. Elizabeth Hooton: a pioneer Quaker

Although readers may not be expecting to see any religious characters in this book, since many of them historically would rather promise that all issues of fairness will be sorted out in the afterlife — pie in the sky when you die — you do have to make an exception for Quakers. The Quakers, aka the Society of Friends, renounce violence and refuse to participate in war. They were in favour of the abolition of slavery long before William Wilberforce took up the cause. They campaign for prison reform and social justice; they were vocal in their support for the anti-capitalist Occupy the City protesters camped on the steps of St Paul's in London.

Quakers refuted the practice espoused by many Puritan groups that to rear children well it is first necessary to "break their spirit." They do not believe in a hierarchy, and so believe in equality of all. Their founder, George Fox of Fenny Drayton in Leicestershire, refused to remove his hat to King Charles II, much to the outrage of onlookers. Quakers refuse to bow or curtsey to anyone, and prefer an egalitarian handshake. They will not swear an oath, since they must speak the truth on all occasions.

One belief that set them apart from other dissenters during and after the Civil War was their belief that every man and woman had the holy spirit inside them. Listening to the God inside — what some of us would term conscience — was all that people need to lead a good life. Other Puritan groups thought that it was enough to replace the high church priests with a Puritan minister, but the Quakers thought that there was no need for any priest or minister to interpret God's message.

Quakers have always welcomed women speakers at their meetings, and the very first convert to Quaker philosophy was a Nottinghamshire woman. When George Fox began to form what became the Quaker doctrine, he left his native Leicestershire to find people who would share his ideals. In 1647, he made his first convert. In the town of Skegby, he met Elizabeth Hooton, a forty-seven-year-old farmer's wife and a member of the Baptist church. Elizabeth welcomed Fox into her home, and became interested in his ideas. They discussed issues at length, and there are those who believe that Elizabeth contributed much to what became the Quaker view of life.

In 1650, Elizabeth decided to leave Skegby and travel round the country spreading the word. She was the first of what became known as the Valiant Sixty, who were all missionaries for the Quaker cause. This demanded not only moral courage, but physical bravery too. In 1651

Elizabeth was imprisoned in Derby for "reproving a priest." Quakers would go into a church — a building George Fox dismissed as a "steeplehouse" — and interrupt the sermon to tell the priest that he was not telling the truth. Another practice used was to listen to the sermon, then get up afterwards to explain to the congregation that they should listen to their inner holy spirit, rather than to the words they had just heard. Elizabeth was imprisoned in York in 1652 for doing exactly that: talking to a congregation after the official service.

In 1660, as Elizabeth was walking down a street in Selston, she met a church minister called Jackson. Without a word being spoken, the man began to beat the sixty-four-year-old woman simply because he knew she was a Quaker.

The word "Quaker" was first used to describe Fox and his followers as an insult. When George Fox was brought before a magistrate named Gervase Bennett in 1650, he told the justice that he should "tremble at the word of God." In an attempt to make fun of Fox, Bennett called him a Quaker. However, the Society of Friends accepted the term with good humour and happily answer to being called Quakers.

The same thing happened in the twentieth century, when the Kaiser called the British forces "that contemptible little army", the soldiers happily referred to themselves as the Old Contemptibles. When the women seeking the vote were mocked by the *Daily Mail* calling them suffragettes — the girlies who want to achieve suffrage — they took on the term with pride. In the miners' strike of 1984–5, the tiny band of Leicestershire striking miners took the insult "the Dirty Thirty" and proudly wore the name.

In 1661, Elizabeth, now a widow, travelled to New England to spread Quaker beliefs in America. This was extremely dangerous. The idea that the Pilgrim Fathers had gone to America in 1620 to establish freedom of worship is a myth. They went to escape persecution for their puritan faith, but then themselves became great persecutors of others. They particularly persecuted Quakers. The puritans believed that they were the elect — God's chosen people, saved by grace with nothing further required except diligent church attendance. They hated the Quakers who pointed out that they had listen to the divine spirit inside themselves and to "become sin-free." The Quakers were whipped and imprisoned. Four Quakers were executed in the Massachusetts Bay colony: William Robinson and Marmaduke Stephenson were hanged in 1659, Mary Dyer in 1660 and William Leddra in 1661. When Mary Dyer was hanged, one unsympathetic member of the Boston court commented that her body should be left to "hang like a flag, as an example to others."

Mary Dyer being taken to the gallows — unknown 19th century artist

It was into this situation that Elizabeth decided to go, accompanied by her friend Joan Brocksop, a Quaker from Derbyshire. They wanted to go to Boston, but it was impossible to go there directly. The governor had passed a law that any ship that took Quakers to New England would be fined £100 and forced to take them back to England. Elizabeth and Joan therefore travelled to Virginia, and then made the difficult overland journey to Boston. They immediately went to visit the imprisoned Quakers. The jailer refused to let them visit, and immediately arrested them. They were taken before John Endicott, the Governor of Massachusetts, who accused them of being witches.

Endicott's previous action in hanging Quakers had met with some disapproval from the authorities in England, so he devised a different method of getting rid of Elizabeth and Joan without killing them directly. After the two Quakers had served their prison sentence, the governor had them transported on a two-day journey into the wilderness, accompanied by men with swords and spears. The two women, both in their sixties, were abandoned in a forest, at the mercy of the elements and wild animals — wolves and bears. Incredibly, they managed somehow to walk out of the wilderness all the way to Rhode Island, where the authorities were less hostile to Quakers. They went from there to the West Indies, but Elizabeth knew that she had to return to Boston. The Boston authorities arrested them once more, they were expelled, and found themselves on a ship to England.

Back in Nottinghamshire, Elizabeth faced another problem. Her property had been seized because of her refusal to pay tithes to the established church. When she refused to swear an oath in court — Quakers would never swear an oath, remember — all her cattle were seized, and she was imprisoned for twelve weeks.

Something had to be done, and Elizabeth decided, with that wonderful Quaker directness, to go to see the king! She needed earthly justice, and she knew the king needed spiritual guidance. She twice managed to track down Charles II to his tennis courts, and told him about what had happened to her in New England and in Nottinghamshire. Although the onlookers were shocked that she refused to kneel or even bow before the monarch, the king was amused by the earnest old Quaker woman. He even went as far as providing her with a signed certificate that entitled her to settle in any British colony.

Armed with this, Elizabeth Hooton returned to New England, only to find that her certificate did not impress the authorities there. As she travelled around spreading the word, this time accompanied by her daughter, she was treated with cruelty everywhere. At Hampton she was imprisoned for protesting when a priest had seized the property of a Quaker. At Dover, she was put in the stocks, then imprisoned. In Cambridge she and her daughter were put in prison for two days and nights without food, then sentenced to be publicly stripped to the waist and whipped in three towns. The two women were dragged through the three towns, a distance of eighty miles, tied to the back of a cart. In Dedham they each received ten lashes, receiving the same punishment at the whipping post in Cambridge, while at Watertown they were thrashed with willow rods, As if this was not sufficiently cruel, the badly-beaten Elizabeth was once more taken into the wilderness and abandoned to die of cold, starvation or by being devoured by wolves. Once more, she survived and walked all the way back to sanctuary in Rhode Island.

Despite being warned that if she returned to Boston, she would be either hanged or branded on the shoulder with an H to mark her as a heretic, she did return again and again, suffering imprisonment and whippings. On one of her visits, she was able to attend the funeral of her old persecutor Governor John Endicott, but when she tried to speak, she was ejected and imprisoned. Later, she was also imprisoned for preaching in Salem and in Braintree. Nothing would prevent this now elderly Quaker from speaking the Quaker philosophy to all she met.

After five years of itinerant preaching, she returned to England, to find that Charles II had now passed draconian laws against Quakerism, and she was incarcerated in Lincoln Prison for "disturbing a congregation." At the age of seventy-one, she travelled with George Fox to Barbados and then on to Jamaica, where she died on 8th January 1672.

George Fox always referred to Elizabeth Hooton, his first convert, as "a very tender woman". But by her moral and physical courage, suffering frequent imprisonments, nine whippings, and twice being taken into the wilderness and abandoned there to perish, Elizabeth showed herself to be a doughty and seasoned campaigner in the cause of the Society of Friends. She proved herself tough as well as tender.

6. George Powe: "a true comrade"

Oswald George Powe — always known as George — was born in Jamaica, in August 1926. His mother, Leonora, was Afro-Caribbean and his father, Richard, was Chinese. George had a twin sister, Daphne, as well as two older sisters and a younger brother. For three years he attended the Chinese School in Kingston, but in 1935 he transferred to St Ann's Elementary School. He completed his education at Kingston Technical School, studying electrical engineering, and in 1944 he lied about his age (he was then seventeen) to join the RAF.

George came to Britain on a troop ship, landing in Scotland. He trained as a radar operator at Yatesbury in Wiltshire, but spent much of his wartime in Devon and Cornwall. By 1945, there were 3,700 Jamaicans serving in the RAF, some as ground crew, others as aircrew.

His impressions of the RAF and of wartime Britain were mixed. Officially, the RAF had a policy of non-discrimination, stating, "All ranks should clearly understand that there is no colour bar in the Royal Air Force," a very progressive attitude for the time, but individuals did not always adhere to this. Many people were friendly, but he did encounter racist remarks and also occasional violence both from civilians and from other RAF personnel.

On one occasion, George and a friend, Rex Thame, were standing talking on the railway station in Penzance waiting for a train to London. A white girl was standing about six or seven feet away. Two white American soldiers came along, and said to the girl, "Are these two niggers molesting you?" The girl said no, but the soldiers raised their voices and repeated, "Are you sure those niggers aren't molesting you?" They continued to loudly abuse George and Rex. George had had enough and asked them, "Who are you calling niggers?" One of the soldiers came across, getting in George's face and spoiling for a fight. He was clearly intending to hand out a beating but before he could start punching, George gave the man a right cross. The man staggered and George used his left foot to trip him over. The two chastened Americans beat a hasty retreat. George had learned that it was not right to cower before aggression. Bullies had to be confronted. You fought if insulted.

In 1940s London, he experienced a great deal of racial discrimination and abuse, and he joined the Communist Party, where he was made very welcome. The CP was very active in fighting against racism.

George was appreciative of the continued education available in the RAF. He recalled that civilian tutors were employed, and many Caribbean servicemen were able to qualify as academics, professionals or craftsmen.

In 1948 he was returned to Jamaica to be demobbed, though he was only there for a short while. After four months, he emigrated as a civilian to live in Britain for the rest of his life. Although George didn't actually come to the UK on the SS Windrush — he came on the SS Orbita — he was very much part of the Windrush generation.

He landed in Liverpool where he lived in a hostel for ex-servicemen. A few months later he moved to the Birmingham area, working as an electrician's mate, a fitter and then as an electrician. While in the West Midlands he met and married Barbara Poole, a cinema usherette. In 1950, they moved to Long Eaton. Although Long Eaton is a proud Derbyshire town, it is only seven miles from Nottingham and has strong links to that city.

In 1960, George joined the Labour Party, and in 1963 he was elected as a councillor on Long Eaton Urban District Council, representing Sawley Ward. Historians believe it probable that George Powe was the first black elected councillor in the country. He was active in the Nottingham Ex-Servicemen's Association, the Anti-Apartheid Movement, the Movement for Colonial Freedom and many other progressive campaigns.

George and Barbara went on to have five children but separated by mutual consent in 1970, and George moved to Lenton, in Nottingham.

George continued to study, and in 1969 he went on a three-year teacher training course at Trent Polytechnic, emerging in 1972 as a qualified maths teacher. He ceased to be George Powe, electrician, and became George Powe, teacher. He continued as a member of the teaching profession until taking early retirement in 1982.

In 1982, George married Jill Westby, a fellow teacher. They had met many years earlier through their mutual membership of CND, where they were both activists, and through a mutual friend, Ken Coates, then leader of Nottingham Labour Party. In fact Jill had been at one time a lodger in Ken's house.

The lives of George and Jill were not restricted to teaching. In 1989 George was elected as a member of Nottinghamshire County Council, representing the Manvers ward of the city. He was a delegate to the Nottingham & District Trades Council and to the Nottingham Racial Equality Council (REC). He was a governor of two Nottingham schools. He was a founder member and secretary of the Afro-Caribbean National Artistic Centre in Nottingham, providing a social centre for senior citizens and women's groups, and providing courses for young unemployed people.

Throughout his life, George fought against colour prejudice and for equality. He successfully campaigned to persuade Raleigh Cycle Company to abandon its colour bar employment policy, and the Raleigh factory became the largest employer of Afro-Caribbean workers in the city. He fought against colour bar attitudes in some Nottingham pubs. He supported forty-four Pakistani workers in their strike over wages and conditions at Crepe Sizes Ltd in Lenton.

If people had a problem understanding how to apply for a visa, George was the man to help, but he also advised on tax returns, debts and divorce procedures. George Powe became the go-to person in Nottingham for anyone needing advice. George would help anyone, whatever their race, to get their rights and to obtain justice.

George died at the age of eighty-seven in 2013.

Among those paying tribute to George was Alan Simpson, the former Nottingham South MP, who said, "He was a really important bridge that stretched across the community and pulled it together." Milton Crosdale, chief executive of Nottingham REC, added, "I always found him to be a gentleman whose concern for others outweighed his personal needs."

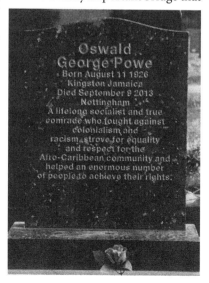

On his gravestone in Wilford Hill cemetery, are the words:

> OSWALD
> GEORGE POWE.
> Born 11 August 1926,
> Kingston, Jamaica.
> Died September 9 2013,
> Nottingham. A lifelong

socialist and true comrade who fought against colonialism and racism, strove for equality and respect for the Afro-Caribbean community and helped an enormous number of people to achieve their rights.

What a fine and fitting tribute to a remarkable man.

7. Alice Wheeldon: framed for conspiracy to murder

Alice Ann Marshall was born on 27th January 1866, the daughter of an engineer who later became an engine driver. At the age of twenty, she married William Wheeldon, a widower fourteen years older than her, a father of two daughters. At various times in his life William described himself as a mechanical engineer, a botanist, and a commercial traveller. Alice and William had four children: Nellie, born in 1888, Harriet — always known as Hettie — born in 1891, William, born in 1892 and Winnie, born in 1893.

To say that Alice Wheeldon was a radical thinker would be an understatement. She was a feminist and a supporter of the women's suffrage movement, although she found its leaders disappointingly half-hearted. She was a member of the Independent Labour Party, a vegetarian, a socialist, a convinced atheist and, above all, a committed pacifist. She was completely opposed to the war that had broken out in 1914. Her attitude to the war contrasted with many of the leaders of the suffrage movement, who supported the war and even gave out white feathers to young men who failed to serve in the army. In this respect, Alice had more in common with Sylvia Pankhurst than with the other members of the Pankhurst family.

Alice was extremely proud of her son William who was a conscientious objector. All conscientious objectors had a hard time. Even the religious COs were treated with scorn, and William — as a political CO — could expect arrest at any time. He left home and went to live with his sister and brother-in-law in Southampton.

Alice lived at 12 Pear Tree Road, Derby; the front of her house was a shop where she sold high quality secondhand clothes. There is evidence that, as well as being a shopkeeper, she had also been a teacher. Living with her was her daughter Hettie, who was an elementary school teacher in Ilkeston. Her older daughter, Nellie, had left home, and her youngest daughter, Winnie, was living in Southampton, where her husband Alfred Mason was a college chemistry lecturer.

The Wheeldon family was opposed to conscription, and the house in Pear Tree Road often sheltered conscientious objectors and army deserters on the run. One resident was a lodger calling himself Alex Gordon. Alex claimed to be a fugitive from military service, and as such he was warmly welcomed into the household.

However, Alice and Harriet were being too trusting: "Alex" was a government agent named William Rickard who had been sent to infiltrate the Wheeldon family. Rickard — he also used the name Francis Vivien — had a chequered history, having been in prison for blackmail, and having spent many years in Broadmoor. However, he was now being used as an agent by PMS2, an intelligence section within the Ministry of Munitions, a department which later became part of MI5 and the Special Branch.

The first member of the Wheeldon family to attract the attention of PMS2 was Nellie, but as things turned out she was never charged with anything, once the attention switched to Alice, Hettie, Winnie and Alfred.

"Alex Gordon" introduced Alice to another man, known as Comrade Bert, supposedly an army deserter and a member of the IWW (Industrial Workers of the World — the Wobblies). But Bert, like Alex Gordon, was not what he seemed. He was Alex's superior officer in the intelligence unit.

To the trusting Derby women, Alex and Bert were both men committed to the causes of pacifism and socialism, giving valuable advice and support to various projects. One of these was a plan put forward by Alex to break into a prison camp in Islington where the political conscientious objectors were being held. Pointing out that the camp had fierce guard dogs, Alex said that it would be necessary to poison the dogs before the prisoners could be rescued. Alice agreed, and wrote to her son-in-law in Southampton to ask if he could obtain curare and strychnine, which, she was told, would be suitable poisons for the task. Alice did feel pangs of regret for "the poor dogs" but she thought that the death of the guard dogs was the unpleasant but necessary price to be paid for the freeing of men wrongly imprisoned.

Alfred and Winnie Mason shared Alice's anti-war views, and Alfred managed to obtain the poison from the laboratory at Hartley University College where he worked. In January 1917 four phials of strychnine and curare were dispatched from Alfred's home in Southampton to the Wheeldon house in Derby.

The police immediately raided the homes of the Wheeldons, where they arrested Alice and a young conscientious objector who was staying there. Alf, who had cycled up to Derby, was also arrested, while his wife Winnie was arrested in Southampton. Hettie was arrested at her school in Ilkeston in front of her class. The four were charged with conspiring to murder the Prime Minister, David Lloyd George, and his minister Arthur Henderson. It was alleged that the poison was to be used on darts to be thrown or fired at the two leading politicians.

At the preliminary hearing at Derby Guildhall, the family were advised by their local solicitor to reserve their defence and not enter a plea. It has been suggested that he probably believed his clients to be guilty. The fact that they did not plead not guilty at this stage may have persuaded others to the same belief.

The main trial was held in London, at the Old Bailey. The prosecution realised that they had a problem. William Rickards, alias Alex Gordon, could not be produced in court. The man had a criminal record and a record of mental illness. He would not make a reliable witness. They had instead to produce Herbert Booth — Comrade Bert — who had met Alice only briefly. Doubts about the strength of the evidence were expressed by Sir Edward Henry, Commissioner of the Metropolitan Police, but he was persuaded to quell his misgivings, and the case went ahead.

It was never going to be an equal battle. The prosecution was led by Sir Frederick ("F.E.") Smith, the Attorney General, and the first witness was "Comrade Bert", now revealed to be Herbert Booth. The prosecution decided that, in order to strengthen their case, it would be necessary to blacken the characters of the Wheeldon family. Much was made of the fact that both Alice and Hettie chose to affirm rather than swear an oath on the Bible. The judge referred to this fact several times, strongly hinting that those who simply affirmed may not be as truthful as those who swore an oath in the traditional manner.

According to Booth, the four accused were hardened political terrorists who had previously tried to kill the Chancellor of the Exchequer in 1915 by sending him a poisoned needle through the post. Just for good measure, he mentioned that they were violent atheists who had once burned down a church at Breadsall, a village to the north of Derby. He then claimed that Alice had told him of a previous plot by members of the Women's Suffrage movement who had spent £300 in an attempt to kill Lloyd George by getting into a hotel where he was staying and driving a nail tipped with poison through the sole of his boot.

Alice, like her fellow accused, pleaded not guilty, and explained that the poison was to be used to kill guard dogs in a project to free prisoners whose only crime was to oppose the war. Her story was not believed, and three of the four accused were found guilty of conspiracy to assassinate the Prime Minister. The exception was Hettie, who was freed. Alice was sentenced to ten years in prison, Alfred Mason to seven years and Winnie to five years. The judge said that Winnie's sentence was lighter only because she had obviously been influenced by her wicked mother.

The accused were never likely to win their case. The prosecution team led by the Attorney General included two King's Counsels, a junior barrister, and dozens of expert witnesses, including leading pathologist Bernard Spilsbury. The defence consisted of only one barrister, Saiyid Riza, and a solicitor. Saiyid Riza was routinely mocked in the press for both his foreign appearance, his mannerisms and his accent. He was variously described in newspaper accounts as being related to the Persian royal family, a "dark-skinned Hindu of Indian origin", a "Mohammedin", and one extremely patronising press description compared him to the fictional and racist *Punch* creation Baboo Hurry Bungsho Jabberjee, BA.

Saiyid Riza made the very telling important point that, although "Comrade Bert" gave evidence, the crown refused to produce the mysterious "Alex Gordon". This meant that the defence was unable to question him about his role in the plot to obtain the strychnine and curare. Alice's statement that it was Alex Gordon who had first asked Alice to provide the poisons could not be put to him.

Alice had sent several letters to her son-in-law on the subject of obtaining poisons. Most of the letters stated clearly that the poisons were for killing guard-dogs but the only letters produced in court were ones where dogs were not specifically mentioned.

The judge, Mr Justice Low, made much of the fact that Alice and her daughters had often used obscenities when talking about the Prime Minister and other government figures. He commented on their foul language, saying that since they had both been teachers, then it obviously followed that elementary education for working-class children was not a good idea!

The prosecution — and indeed the judge — frequently asked questions which led Alice to agree that she regarded Arthur Henderson as a traitor to the working class, that she hated Lloyd George and that she thought it would be a good thing if his career came to an end. She admitted once saying that "George of Buckingham Palace" was another man that deserved to be done in, though she added that she had only said it "in my bitterness," and had not meant it literally.

The whole trial was one-sided, and it is not surprising that the jury took only thirty minutes to reach its verdict. The atmosphere of wartime

Britain was one of suspicion and rumour. German spies were seen everywhere. A trial in 1916 was interrupted when a *Times* reporter was accused of taking notes in German style writing, though it later turned out that he was using an old form of shorthand. A pro-German organisation known as the Hidden Hand was said to be sapping the fighting spirit of the British forces by spreading lesbianism and homosexuality.

This atmosphere, plus the fact that every town in England had lost husbands and sons in the desperate massacres of the trenches, meant that the trial of the Wheeldon family was not going to be even-handed.

After the trial was over, but before the court dispersed, the judge gave permission for Mrs Emmeline Pankhurst, the women's suffrage leader, to make a statement. In it, Mrs Pankhurst stated that the Women's Political and Social Union had never offered money for an attempt on the life of Lloyd George, and would never countenance the taking of any human life. Edward Garner, in his book, *Was You Ever In Dovedale?* takes the view that this statement might have been useful to Alice Wheeldon's case and should have been heard earlier, during the trial.

It seems to me that Alice Wheeldon, about to start a ten-year sentence, might have heard the words of the statement with some cynicism. She was already disillusioned with the way that the suffragists' leaders had ceased their political activities to support the war. Now, here was Mrs Pankhurst come to denounce the more radical of the feminist activists, those who opposed the war.

After the verdict, Alice and Winnie were sent to Holloway Prison, and Alfred to Wandsworth. Their right to appeal was dismissed. Alice and Winnie were later transferred to Aylesbury Prison, where Alice began a campaign of non-cooperation including several periods of hunger strike. Attempts were made to force-feed her but she resisted these vigorously. She was also accused of encouraging fellow prisoners to ignore the prison rules and refused to wear prison uniform. Winnie remained at Aylesbury, but Alice was returned to Holloway, where her health deteriorated rapidly. The governor there was afraid that the authorities might be planning to release Alice and advised against it, stating, that she was "a deep, dangerous, malicious, scheming woman."

However, word came down from above — from Lloyd George himself — that Alice Wheeldon must not be allowed to die in prison. She was released in late December 1917. Alf and Winnie Mason were released, again at the instigation of Lloyd George, in January 1918.

The trial, held at the Old Bailey, was a national sensation at the time, but it is now widely accepted that there was no plot to assassinate the Prime Minister. The authorities were anxious to discredit those who were providing underground help for conscientious objectors to evade imprisonment, and sent in two spies — William Rickards and Herbert Booth — to first infiltrate and then to subvert the Wheeldon activities. It is probable that the idea of obtaining poison first came from one of these two agents. It is certain that its use was to be for poisoning guard dogs, and that the fantastic plot to assassinate Lloyd George was a fiction devised either by the unreliable William Rickards or by others higher up in the shadowy secret intelligence ranks.

It is possible that Lloyd George realised this. He may have released Alice because he feared a public outcry if she died in prison, but his decision to release her daughter and son-in-law might indicate that the Prime Minister knew that the whole trial had been a sham. On his express orders a Home Office review was held in 1919, and it was decided that the three had been convicted on dubious evidence. Although Alice was released, she had been so weakened by her treatment in prison — including hard labour and force-feeding during hunger strikes — that she died in February 1919 in the national Spanish flu epidemic. She was buried in an unmarked grave in Derby's Nottingham Road cemetery.

Hettie Wheeldon married Arthur MacManus, a committed anti-war activist, but she died in November 1920. The rest of the family spread all over the world. Nellie went to Canada, and for a long time local historians believed that Alf and Winnie moved to Australia. However, recent evidence has emerged that shows that it was actually their son Peter who emigrated to Australia. It would seem probable, therefore, that Winnie and Alfred Mason lived somewhere in England for the rest of their lives.

Alice's son-in-law Arthur became a founding member and the first chair of the Communist Party of Great Britain; following his death in London in 1927, he had the honour of having his remains placed in the Kremlin Wall. Alice's son William Wheeldon had a very different end. He too joined the CPGB. He went to live in Russia, and became a translator for the Comintern. As a dedicated admirer of Leon Trotsky, he was executed by firing squad in 1937 in a Stalinist purge.

William Rickards, the government spy and agent provocateur, emigrated to South Africa, in an uncanny replica of the final destination of Oliver the Spy in the case of the Pentrich Rising a hundred years earlier.

The whole event was cloaked in mystery and double-dealing. The shadowy figures of "Comrade Bert" and "Alex Gordon", the underhand machinations of the secret service and the inclusion of the office of the Prime Minister all combine to make an evil-smelling concoction of confusion and intrigue.

If the authorities' original intention was to silence Alice Wheeldon and to wipe out all public memory of her existence and her ideals, it is pleasing to note that they failed. *A Plot To Kill Lloyd George*, a BBC television programme broadcast in 1983, investigated the events of 1916–17, with Brenda Bruce recreating the role of Alice Wheeldon. This programme came to the conclusion that there was a conspiracy, but it was one to frame the Wheeldon family, rather than one to assassinate the Prime Minister. In 1988, the case was recreated on the stage in a play called *The Friends of Alice Wheeldon* by Sheila Rowbotham. The case has now been revisited in the book *The Plot to Kill Lloyd George* by Nicola Rippon.

In Derby today there is a campaign to clear the name of the Wheeldon and Mason families. In the view of Dr Nick Hiley of the University of Kent, speaking to a meeting of the Derby People's History group in 2011, it is not enough to find that the evidence was insufficient to prove their guilt. The point is not to find the accusation of conspiracy to murder unproven. It is to clear the names of four totally innocent people.

Among those supporting the campaign are Australian citizens Chloe and Deidre Mason. They are the granddaughters of Alfred and Winnie Mason, the great-granddaughters of Alice Wheeldon. In an email Chloe Mason told me, "We are delighted by the campaign."

8. Elizabeth Heyrick: an "immediate" anti-slavery abolitionist

Elizabeth Heyrick was widowed in 1875 at the age of twenty-five, when her husband John died of a heart attack. Elizabeth Coltman had married John Heyrick at the age of seventeen, after a brief courtship. John's jealous nature and fiery temperament caused Elizabeth some problems, especially when he isolated her from her family. At the time of the marriage John was a town clerk, but he then enlisted in the 15th Light Dragoons, and took his wife with him to live in army quarters in various parts of England and Ireland. Elizabeth was a member of the Society of Friends, the peace-loving Quakers, which must have been extremely unusual for the wife of a soldier. The couple later returned to their Leicester home, situated near Bow Bridge, and John became a captain in the Leicester Yeomanry.

After John's death, Elizabeth, now a young widow with no children, returned to live at the home of her parents. Her father was a manufacturer of worsted, and her mother was a poet and literary reviewer. Elizabeth opened a school in her former marital home, but teaching was only one part of her life.

She had read all of the works of Tom Paine, and was a strong supporter of his ideas. She campaigned for prison reform, better treatment of vagrants, higher wages for workers and a reduction in the length of the working day. She became a prison visitor, and would often pay the fines of men imprisoned for poaching. She also supported a strike of Leicester weavers, despite the fact that her brother was an employer in that trade. She was the author of more than twenty political pamphlets supporting radical causes.

Elizabeth was not only a woman of undoubted moral courage. She had always hated the "sport" of bull-baiting, where a pack of hungry dogs would be set on a bull in a fight to the death, to the delight of a crowd of cheering spectators. On one occasion, while visiting Bonsall in Derbyshire, she showed enormous physical courage by halting a bull-baiting contest. She bought the bull that was about to be baited, and hid it in a nearby cottage until the angry crowd, deprived of their fun, eventually dispersed.

Her main cause, however, was the abolition of slavery. Many abolitionists, including William Wilberforce and his Anti-Slavery Society, were arguing for a gradualist reform. They wanted to stop the practice of transporting slaves from Africa to the Americas, but were content to leave existing slaves to their life of slavery. They argued that, as those slaves grew old and eventually died, that would solve the problem, and slavery would cease. The plight of the men, women and children still living out their whole lives subject to the cruelty and obscenity of slavery were ignored by these gradualists. Also, of course, any children born to existing slaves would become slaves themselves.

In her 1824 pamphlet *Immediate Not Gradual Abolition*, Elizabeth called for the immediate emancipation of all slaves in the British colonies. She strongly attacked "the slow, cautious, accommodating measures" of Wilberforce and his friends, calling their position a "masterpiece of satanic policy." She accused them of wishing to accommodate the feelings and views of the wealthy slave-owners, rather than tackling the real evil of slavery.

Her pamphlet was widely read and discussed. William Wilberforce was outraged and instructed that his followers should not appear on the same platform as Heyrick and those who shared her views.

It wasn't just the arguments of the immediate abolitionists that appalled him. It was the fact that Elizabeth and many of her supporters were women. Writing to his friend Thomas Babington of Rothley, he stated: "For ladies to meet, to publish, to go from house to house stirring up petitions — these appear to me proceedings unsuited to the female character as delineated in scripture."

His pompous and pious attitudes gathered less public approval than the arguments put forward by Elizabeth Heyrick and her friends. George Stephen argued that the women "formed the cement of the anti-slavery building — without their aid we never should have kept standing." Thomas Clarkson, one of Wilberforce's colleagues in the Anti-Slavery Society, stated that women should have a role in public life.

Elizabeth, her sister Mary Ann, and a fellow-campaigner Suzanna Watts launched an anti-slavery periodical *The Hummingbird*.

Elizabeth didn't confine her anti-slavery work to writing and publishing. Why just petition Parliament, she argued, when we can do things for ourselves more effectively and more speedily? In Leicester, she took direct action by organising a boycott of sugar produced on the West Indian slave plantations. Together with Suzanna Watts, she visited grocers throughout the city and urged them not to sell sugar produced by slavery. Hundreds of Leicester families stopped buying West Indian sugar, much to the anger of the Leicester local press.

These sugar boycotts soon spread to other parts of the country, and gained wide support among abolitionists. Independent women's groups were set up in Leicester, Nottingham, Birmingham, Norwich, London, Manchester, Darlington and Glasgow, to support immediate and complete abolition of slavery. The Birmingham group stated that they would stop paying their annual £50 affiliation fee to the official Anti-Slavery body unless it abandoned its gradualist approach.

In 1830, at the annual conference of the Anti-Slavery Society, it was agreed to drop the words "gradual abolition" from its constitution. Moreover, it agreed to support the women's plan for a new campaign to bring about immediate abolition. Wilberforce and his friends had been brought round, if somewhat reluctantly, to the position advocated by Elizabeth Heyrick in her pamphlets.

Sadly, Elizabeth died in 1831, two years before the Abolition of Slavery Act was passed by Parliament. Although she did not live to see her work finally accomplished, Elizabeth and her friends had made abolition possible. Their argument for immediate emancipation had triumphed over the gradualist attitudes of William Wilberforce. It is somewhat ironic that the name of William Wilberforce is the one that is remembered and the name of Elizabeth Heyrick that is often neglected.

9. Bas Barker: a Chesterfield legend

Bas was born on 16th Sept 1910 in Holmewood, a mining village near Chesterfield. His dad, John, was a face worker at Williamthorpe Colliery. John didn't like the fact that the pit management was in charge of everything in the village — the co-op, the chapel, the miners' homes — so he moved out of the company house to live in Grassmoor. John was entirely self-taught, organising a reading group of miners who would pass books between themselves. He was originally an active Methodist but grew disillusioned with religion during WWI, asking himself how English and German clergy were each praying for victory, asking their God to support their cause. He decided that only secular politics would serve the cause of the working man, and concentrated his efforts in the Labour Party and the unions.

Like his father, Bas was an avid reader, particularly enjoying the works of Charles Dickens and the American socialist writer Jack London. At the age of sixteen, Bas joined the Communist Party. As he was the only local member of that age, he was allowed to join the adult section, rather than the Young Communist League.

At the same time, he became involved in the General Strike of 1926. The local Trades Council set up the strike headquarters in the Miners Welfare in Chesterfield. One of his comrades there was Vin Williams, who was arrested for sedition. His "crime" was to write an article in the strike broadsheet, reporting on the rumour that some regiments of soldiers had refused to take action against strikers. Vin commented that "blood was thicker than water," and urged soldiers not to turn against their fellow working men. Vin was arrested, taken to court where he was found guilty, fined £5 and given a two-month prison sentence.

Although a CP member, Bas continued to campaign to get a Labour MP elected locally. He spoke on Labour Party platforms and was even on the Constituency Labour Party executive. Bas harked back to the time when any socialist was welcome at Labour Party meetings, an attitude that continued in Chesterfield even when the national Labour Party began to proscribe people. He was delighted when George Benson was elected in 1929 as Chesterfield's first ever Labour MP, but became disillusioned by the treachery of Labour leader Ramsay MacDonald who formed a National Government with Stanley Baldwin. The seat was lost in 1931. In 1933, there was a by-election in the neighbouring Clay Cross constituency and the national Labour Party imposed a candidate. This was Arthur Henderson, the Labour Party general secretary, a known right-winger. The Communist Party ran their own candidate — Harry Pollitt — and Bas was very active in supporting him.

Although Bas hadn't enjoyed school, he was determined to improve his education and he won a scholarship for a two-week summer school at Balliot College, Oxford. In 1931, as the son of a miner, he won a Miners' Welfare scholarship which entitled him to attend a course at Nottingham University for two days a week. In this two-year course, he studied economics, industrial history and logic.

He became an activist in the National Unemployed Workers Movement, and in 1935, the Communist Party suggested that he should become a full-time student at the Lenin School in Moscow. This was a big step for a young man who had hardly been away from home at all, but Bas decided to go. He travelled from London docks on a ship to Leningrad, and then by train to Moscow. At the Lenin School he studied the theory, history and practice of Marxism. His fellow students came from all over the world — Ireland, America, Germany, France, Australia — a thoroughly international mix. Among the people he met there were Chou-en Lai, Maurice Thorez and Palmiro Togliatti, leaders of the party in China, France and Italy respectively.

On his return to the UK in 1937, Bas became the full-time CP organiser for Sheffield, a post he took over from Jock Kane, and in 1939, he married Beryl, a Sheffield girl whose family had been involved in the labour movement in that city for generations.

Earlier in 1939, Bas had taken a job back in Chesterfield, at the Sheepbridge Stokes engineering works. When he'd been there for two or three weeks, the general manager sent for Bas and told him that he'd received a somewhat alarming letter from the Sheffield police. This stated that Basil Barker was a very dangerous individual, who had probably taken a job at the engineering works in order to blow it up! Bas had obviously had a few run-ins with the Sheffield police while organizing demonstrations, but this vindictive letter was over the top. The manager believed Basil's side of things and kept him on. He did suggest that Bas went onto permanent days, where there was more supervision. This left Bas with a dilemma. Working permanent days was much better than his current shift system of two weeks on days, followed by two weeks on nights. Working on days gave him more time to attend meetings in the evening. Despite this, Bas argued that it was unfair to put him on the highly desirable days-only shift, and, after six months, he was put back on shifts on a probationary basis. Trial period or not, Bas remained working at Sheepbridge Stokes for the next thirty-eight years. As an active member of the Amalgamated Engineering Union, he was soon elected as union convenor, a post he kept for the whole of his working life.

During the war, Sheepbridge Stokes manufactured parts for the Merlin aircraft engines used in Spitfires. They were a sub-contractor for Rolls Royce, who were anxious for the Chesterfield engineers to increase production, if possible by 100%. The management said this was completely impossible, but asked Bas for his opinion. Bas suggested that workers from each section involved should be invited to comment on how their section could increase output. Then the workers could together come up with a figure of units that could be produced. This revolutionary concept — workers using their shop-floor knowledge of production to decide what could be done, rather than having a target imposed by management — was put into practice. Workers were kept informed through regular canteen meetings and a "wall newspaper". Bas made sure that their efforts were not used to lower the piecework wages, and that other wages within the factory were not adversely affected. What Rolls Royce had needed was 2000 units every week and the workers at Sheepbridge Stokes achieved this. Bas had made his point. The men could achieve what management had said was impossible.

In the post-war period, Bas became involved in the international peace movement. In 1949 he attended a peace conference in East Berlin, and a second in Paris in 1950. He was an organizer for a third conference to be held in Sheffield the following year. Bas arranged for the delegates from all over the world to be housed in the homes of ordinary citizens in Sheffield and Chesterfield. Among the early arrivals were Pablo Picasso, French writer Henri Barbusse, and Russian composer Aram Khachaturian. Bas had arranged for the delegates to eat their meals at a local restaurant where the owner was sympathetic, and he took this group for a meal there. During the meal, Picasso drew the dove of peace emblem on the menu, added a greeting, signed it and presented it to Bas. The restaurant manager saw it and asked Bas if he could get Picasso to do one for him. Bas was reluctant to pester the artist, and gave the man his own. Bas had never even considered the monetary value of a signed Picasso drawing — he had never put any store in material wealth — but I believe Beryl reminded Bas of this for decades afterwards, saying that it was "one sacrifice too many!"

This conference was being held at the height of the Cold War, where any contact with Russia and Eastern Europe was regarded with the utmost suspicion by the government. There was right-wing press hysteria about "dangerous foreign Reds" being allowed to come to Sheffield. At the last moment, Clement Attlee, the Labour Prime Minister, banned delegates from abroad from attending, thus destroying the whole conference, which moved to Warsaw instead. In Bas's own words, "The banning added an extra dimension to the developing Cold War and deepened the split between East and West, with the peace movement suffering a setback, the responsibility for which lay largely with the British Labour government. So embittered were they in their attitude towards the progressive movement that they even preferred to use the forces of state to defeat the aims that the peace movement was trying to achieve. It is a contribution that should be to the eternal shame of the labour movement."

In the 1950 general election, Bas Barker made a big decision. He was asked by the CP to stand for Parliament in the Chesterfield constituency, and agreed to do so. He was the only CP parliamentary candidate ever to stand in Chesterfield. The sitting Labour MP was George Benson, a right winger, a former estate agent. The Tory candidate was Andrew Cavendish, the future Duke of Devonshire, and there was also a Liberal candidate, J. O'Neill. At one meeting, organized by the Transport and General Workers Union in St Helen's pub in Chesterfield, all four candidates were there to speak. When Andrew Cavendish commented that he was finding the whole election process exhausting and asked Bas how he found the strength to keep going, Bas replied that he found it easy as was used to working for a living!

One of Bas's supporters, who spoke at many of his election meetings, was a vicar, the Reverend Alan Ecclestone, who combined his Christian beliefs with Communist Party membership. Despite this endorsement, Bas received a great deal of hate mail — saying that he, his wife and his children all deserved to die in horrible agony — from people describing themselves as Christians.

Bas stood in order to point out that the Labour government wanted to impose economies to keep the country "so-called solvent," to run the capitalist system better than the Tories. Bas preferred to campaign for peace and against developing nuclear weapons, to improve wages, working conditions, housing and social services. Although he got a great deal of groundswell support and had some very well-attended meetings, this did not translate into votes. The people of Chesterfield, many of them miners, decided that they would stick with their normal practice and re-elect the Labour MP.

This election was a one-off though. In most elections Bas concentrated on trying to ensure that the Labour Party selected a good socialist candidate, and worked to make sure that candidate was elected. He thought he'd achieved both in 1964, when Eric Varley was chosen to fight the seat. Eric had good left-wing credentials, but Bas was disappointed when the new MP took a position as Harold Wilson's parliamentary private secretary, thus losing his ability to speak for the left in Parliament. Varley became an establishment Labour figure, and ended up in the cabinet, before leaving political life in 1984 to become chairman of a private company.

To the delight of Bas — and many others — the candidate chosen to fight the by-election in Chesterfield was Tony Benn. The adoption of Tony Benn reinvigorated the left in Chesterfield. There were mass turnouts for meetings where he was speaking, and activists from all over the country turned out to support his candidature. There was massive coverage in the press — much of it hostile — and on television. Bas reported, "The campaign itself was fought out at grass roots level in the streets, the factories, the market place, the pubs and the clubs. The issues were taken to the people." The election of Tony Benn as MP for Chesterfield was an indication of the level of political debate and socialist activity present in the town.

Bas Barker was always at the centre of that activity. He was president of the Chesterfield Trades Council, as well as president of the Chesterfield district committee of the Amalgamated Engineering Union. He was chairman of the governors of Chesterfield College. He fought on the side of the miners — Chesterfield was a mining town — during the year-long miners' strike of 1984–85. He was an active participant in organizing the annual May Day celebrations. The People's May Day, held in Chesterfield on the first Saturday in May, became the largest event of its kind in the country, attracting more people than similar events in Glasgow or London. It is the high spot in the calendar of the town.

Chesterfield rewarded Bas by granting him the freedom of the borough. Over a century, the award had been given to just twenty-five people, all of them connected to local businesses or to the council. The decision to give the award to Bas Barker was unique — a real break with that tradition. It had never gone to a trades unionist, let alone to a member of the Communist Party. Bas thought about the offer. His attitude to establishment honours was antagonistic. However, he decided that this particular one was different, it was being given in recognition of his unwavering integrity and his contribution to the labour movement within the town. Any lingering doubts he may have had were extinguished when the local Tories publicly opposed the award!

A second honour followed six years later when Derbyshire County Council published his autobiography *Free But Not Easy* in 1989. Bas Barker died in February 1994 at the age of eighty-three, but his name is still remembered and respected in Chesterfield.

10. Geoffrey Trease: Bows Against the Barons

No book about radical heroes of the East Midlands would be complete without a mention of Robin Hood. Yes, I do realize he is a mythical figure, but he is also a legend. And a community can be judged by its legends and folk heroes. General Ludd was a legend, as was Captain Swing.

Obviously, I am not thinking of the pathetic Hollywood creation of a dispossessed aristocratic Robin Hood, fighting to reclaim his status. The most amusing and annoying versions of that particular storyline have Richard I — Richard Coeur de Lion — riding in during the finale to restore Robin Hood to his lands and title. Richard I in England? That would be once in a blue moon. Richard I speaking English? That never happened.

The Robin Hood legend with more authenticity is the earlier one of a man of the people fighting against the aristocrat landlords and the monarchy. When Walter Raleigh was on trial for treason in 1603, he said he was not so mad as to make himself "a Robin Hood, a Wat Tyler, a Kett or a Jack Cade." Wat Tyler was the leader of the 1381 Peasants' Revolt. Jack Cade led a revolt in Kent against the oppression, injustice and corruption of the barons in 1450. Robert Kett, a Wymondham tanner, led a struggle in Norfolk to reclaim common land for the people in 1549.

It is therefore evident from Raleigh's statement that in 1603, Robin Hood was regarded as a rebel in the same mould as Wat Tyler, Robert Kett and Jack Cade. He was thought of as a leader of an armed revolt against authority, a true revolutionary.

An author who returned to this view of the local folk hero was Nottingham-born Geoffrey Trease. In *Bows Against the Barons*, a children's book written in 1934, he portrays Robin as a leader of a rebellion.

The book tells the story of Dickon, a sixteen-year-old serf, and opens with him being whipped by the bailiff for failing to turn up for work on time, then bullied by the priest over the tithe he must pay. His problems get worse that night when deer from the nearby forest get into his garden and damage the meagre crops. Driving them out, he kills one of them. To escape the inevitable punishment for killing a king's deer — having an ear cut off — he hides the dead stag, picks up his bow and his knife and flees into Sherwood Forest.

Well into the forest, Dickon hides as four mounted men, wearing the livery of a baron from the far side of the forest, ride past. They are laughing about the fruit borne by the trees. After they have gone he sees that the "fruit" they referred to was the remains of a hanged man, suspended above him.

He travels on, walking further than he has ever walked before, before settling down to sleep. He wakes to find a forest rebel standing over him, demanding to know who he is. Dickon tells his story, and the man says he will take him to meet Robin Hood and the other rebels, adding that if he turns out to be a spy for the foresters, he'll be strung up.

In a village made up of cave houses and camouflaged log huts, the boy meets Robin Hood and his fellow outlaws. At first Dickon is disappointed — Robin is older than he expected — but then he realized that "he was something bigger and stronger than any of the men who made working men kneel as they passed." After proving his skill with a bow and arrow, the boy is accepted into the band of rebels, but Robin gently reprimands the boy for calling him sir, saying, "We're all equal in Sherwood — comrades."

A few weeks later, Robin sends Dickon — disguised as an apprentice — into the town of Nottingham, with a message for weaver Thomas Pole. That night, Dickon accompanies the weaver to a meeting, held in the caves beneath the town, where a score of working men are planning a protest the next day. Dickon is initially shocked to hear the king criticised, but then realizes that it is true: the king and the barons are equally oppressors of the people. He is also surprised when a Nottingham bridlesmith states that there are poor Normans as well as poor Saxons, Nottingham being a mixed town, and they should fight together. "It isn't Normans against Saxons, it's masters against men."

The next day, Dickon finds himself caught up in a crowd of working men who are demanding that the sheriff releases wrongfully imprisoned men from the jail. The sheriff appears with a double rank of pikemen, who attack the crowd, but Robin Hood and the forest rebels appear, and use their arrows to hold back the sheriff's men. As the crowd manages to break open the jail and free the prisoners, armed horsemen from Nottingham Castle ride in to quell the citizens, and the crowd scatters.

Dickon's subsequent misadventures include getting completely lost in the subterranean caves beneath Nottingham, and later being captured by a band of the king's forest wardens. He manages to find his way out of the caves through a mixture of luck and gritty determination. His rescue from the wardens occurs by a combination of action from a blacksmith, who leads villagers against the king's men, and the efforts of a blind harper, who turns out to be Alan-a-Dale, one of the forest rebels, in disguise.

Dickon returns to the forest. A few days later, Robin hears that soldiers are being sent to punish the villagers who had helped Dickon escape. Although there are only twenty men in the punishment squad — they intend to hang the blacksmith and whip and fine the rest of the villagers — they are accompanied by a hundred soldiers on their way to York. The fifty forest rebels mount an ambush, using their archery skills to bring down the mounted soldiers. The rebels are victorious; many of the soldiers are killed and the rest flee back to Nottingham. When Robin Hood orders his men to collect all the weapons and armour, Dickon is puzzled as lances and chainmail are not items the rebels have ever used. Robin sends the captured weapons to the blacksmith, to hide "until the day".

In a later chapter, *A Dream for England*, Robin shares his beliefs. At a campfire meeting, he tells his comrades, "All men are equal in the forest. They should be equal in the whole world. They should work for themselves and each other — not for some master set over them. Let the ploughman plough for all and the weaver weave for all — but let no lord step in to steal the harvest and no merchant prince to take the cloth." He continues, "There must be an end to serfdom! An end of tolls and tithes, and dues and forced service. No more castles, no more hired cut-throats in livery, no more war service, no barons, no king!"

As the forest rebels take up the cry, "No barons, no king!" Robin reveals his plan, that one day they will take part in a rising of serfs in the country and workmen in the towns. It will start in Sherwood, in midwinter when it will be hard for other barons to send troops to Nottingham, and will then spread all over the land.

At Christmas, Robin sends a disguised Dickon — his hair bleached and curled like that of a page — into D'Eyncourt Castle, the home of his former master, Sir Rolf. He is to observe the castle's fortifications and find its weak points. However, his disguise is rumbled by the other pages and he is forced to hide in the chapel. He hides high on the beams, and when his pursuers have gone, he manages to escape and return to Sherwood Forest.

When Dickon reports that the castle defences have no weak points, Robin adjusts his plan. After the twelve days of Christmas are over, and the visiting barons and their retinues have left the castle, ten of Robin's men gain access in various disguises: one is a peasant selling eggs, others join a party of players and storytellers. All have mail and swords under their clothing. Dickon gets in as a humpbacked boy carrying a huge load of firewood, inside which are longbows and arrows. One by one they make their way to the chapel and climb onto the high beams, just as Dickon had done previously.

When night comes, the rebels hear Robin Hood's horn sounding from outside the castle: the attack has begun. As soldiers pour out across the courtyard, arrows from the rebels in the chapel rain down on them. The rebels gain access to the keep, managing to lock themselves in and to lower the portcullis. Once out on the battlements, they see soldiers on the outer ramparts, preparing to pour boiling oil and stones onto the attackers. From their vantage points the rebels are able to fire arrows at the soldiers. As the soldiers turn their crossbow fire on the rebels in the keep, armed rebel serfs manage to scale the walls and enter the castle. Notwithstanding their small numbers, the serfs raise the portcullis and lower the drawbridge enabling Robin and the main body of besiegers to enter the castle. Hand to hand combat ensues, and Dickon fights and kills his old torturer, the bailiff. The battle ends with Sir Rolf D'Eyncourt dead, and the castle in flames.

The outlaws return to Sherwood, and plan an even greater victory: the capture of Nottingham Castle itself.

Serfs from all over Nottinghamshire rally to Robin's call to rebel, and the authorities become increasingly alarmed and desperate. First the townspeople of Nottingham are ruthlessly crushed and their leaders hanged. Word is sent out to other barons for help and six thousand soldiers are amassed in the town, with a further five thousand in Newark, twenty miles to the northeast. The archbishops are ordered to proclaim in all their churches that the rebellion is against God's will. As news arrives that manor house after manor house has fallen to the rebels, it is ordered that no written record — secular or religious — of the rebellion is to be made. Any reference to it must be wiped out of history.

When Robin sees thousands of soldiers being marched north, he concludes that Nottingham Castle is now open for the rebels to attack. The townspeople will open the gates of the town and the castle can be taken. The rebel army, armed with captured swords, lances and axes, marches towards Nottingham. Alan rides ahead with three hundred men on horseback, the rest follow on foot. Little John and Dickon ride with the rest of the mounted men to form the rearguard. Other forest rebels with their bows guard the flanks, looking out for signs of ambush.

Suddenly the rearguard is attacked by the Newark soldiers, and a terrible battle ensues. The barons and knights are certain that they can teach this rabble of ploughboys a lesson, but the grit and determination of the serfs, plus the arrows from Robin's bowmen, drive them back. Then the soldiers last seen riding north reappear and the rebels are caught in a pincer movement between the two armies. News comes from Nottingham that the workers there have been put down and the gates remain locked. They are now in a fight to the death.

Despite fighting valiantly, the rebels are defeated. Many are slain, but a few straggling groups manage to get away. One such group of men, including Little John, Dickon, and a wounded Robin Hood, make their way back into the forest, then head north into Yorkshire. They take the injured Robin to the abbey at Kirklees, where they ask the nuns to dress his wounds. The prioress immediately recognizes the rebel leader and remembers the huge bounty on his head. Robin is admitted to the abbey, but the other men have to remain outside. To the horror of some of the nuns, the prioress bleeds the injured leader time and time again, until he is dying.

Realising what is happening, Robin asks the prioress if he can have his bow and an arrow to fire from the window. He gives the prioress a cock-and-bull story about wanting to be buried where the arrow lands, while in fact knowing that the men will recognize it as a call for help. Thinking that the outlaw will never be buried — he will be hanged, drawn and quartered and his head stuck on a spike — the prioress agrees.

The rebels see the arrow, and break into the abbey, only to find their leader already dead. He is buried secretly where the barons and king will never find him, and they burn down the abbey in revenge. The few remaining rebels split up, one heading for Ireland, others for all parts of the country. Little John and Dickon head for Hathersage in North Derbyshire, Little John's native village. All agree that they will continue to spread the dream the England could one day be free of masters. No barons, no king.

Bows Against the Barons was published in 1934 to a varied response. In some places it was prescribed, in others it was proscribed. In Russia it was recommended that every school should have a copy, while in colonial India it was banned. The response in the UK was mixed. Some critics saw it as a breath of fresh air, breaking way from the established tradition of children's books set in a romantic "Merrie England." Others condemned it as communist propaganda, though Geoffrey Trease was never a member of the Communist Party. In his autobiography, *A Whiff of Burnt Boats*, he was later to write, "I never seriously considered joining the Communist Party. Ingenuous I might be, but I noticed what happened to individuals who left the party on a sincere difference of opinion. It is fair to say that no-one, either in England or Russia, ever asked me to join. Left-wing idealists, I came to realize, were of more use outside."

Between 1934 and 1997, Geoffrey Trease went on to write over a hundred historical novels for children, including *Comrades for the Charter* (also published in 1934), *Cue for Treason* (set in Tudor England), *Popinjay Stairs* (set in the time of Samuel Pepys) *The Hills of Varna*, *No Boats on Bannermere*, *The Crown of Violet*, *A Thousand for Sicily*, *The Iron Czar*, and *Danger in the Wings*.

Today he is regarded by readers and by critics with affection and respect. In an article entitled "Children's Historical Fiction: a Personal Assessment", Belinda Copson, the co-editor of the children's literature journal *Folly Magazine*, writes, "Geoffrey Trease changed all existing expectations of what children's historical fiction could and should be. His stories were adventures, full of plot and interest, but always firmly in the carefully researched setting of an actual historical event. The history itself was important, not just a light background, but integral to the development of the plot."

Belinda Copson also makes the point that he wrote books to feature both sexes, although this is not true of *Bows Against the Barons*, which has no main female characters. In subsequent books, girls do play a leading role.

Cue For Treason is set in Elizabethan England at the end of the sixteenth century. Two young runaways, Kit and Peter, become boy actors, at first on the road with a company of travelling players, and later in London, where they are befriended by William Shakespeare. During the course of the novel, Kit turns out to be a young woman in disguise, running away from an arranged marriage.

In *The Hills of Varna*, a young Italian woman disguises herself as a boy and joins an expelled Cambridge student on his quest in the sixteenth-century Balkans to discover a lost Greek play manuscript. As in *The Hills of Varna* and *Cue for Treason*, the boy hero of *The Crown of*

Violet befriends a spirited, convention-defying girl who plays a vital role in the adventure.

In his obituary in 1998, Ann Thwaite wrote, "From the beginning, Trease did away with gadzookery and varlets crying 'Zounds' or 'Prithee'. His Sherwood outlaws spoke as ordinary human beings. He was a compulsive writer. It gave him some satisfaction to celebrate his hundredth book and to look at the long shelves of his lifetime's work, many of the titles translated into a wide variety of languages. It is certainly as a storyteller — and as a good man — that he will be long remembered."

Trease's books were always well-researched, and he rarely made mistakes. However, he used to tell one tale against himself. In one story, set in Anglo-Saxon England, his heroes travel along the Fosse Way. The author studied maps of Roman Britain to get the historical geography correct, but he does have them eating rabbit meat. This was not noticed by his publisher or by any of the critics, but a young lad from Aberdeen wrote to him, pointing out that rabbits were actually introduced into England by the Normans. Strangely, the origin of rabbits in Britain is still being debated.

Geoffrey Trease was the author of many historical novels for children, but it is for restoring the unromanticised rebel-leader version of Robin Hood — the one referred to by Walter Raleigh — that I will always admire him. I didn't come across *Bows Against the Barons* until I was in my thirties. I wish I had read it as a child. It should be on every child's reading list.

11. Avtar Sadiq: poet and IWA activist

Avtar Singh Sadiq came to Leicester at the age of twenty-three, and lived in that city from 1964 until his death in 2018. He was a leading figure in the Indian Workers' Association (GB), becoming its General Secretary in 1988. In 1993 he became the national president of the IWA and held that office for nine years.

He was born in 1941 in the village of Chak, which is now in Pakistan. When the 1947 partition took place, dividing the country into India and Pakistan, there was much bloodshed and many atrocities were committed. Huge numbers of refugees were forced to flee, Muslims heading for Pakistan, and Hindus and Sikhs and secularists heading for India. Avtar's parents managed to reach their original home in East Punjab. Avtar's mother died when he was eleven years old, and his father remarried. Although his stepmother did not treat him well, he did get on well with his stepbrothers and stepsisters.

In 1961, he graduated from DAV (Dayanand Ayur Vedic) College in Hoshiarpur, then completed a postgraduate teacher training course. He was already a highly respected poet and writer, as well as a qualified teacher, when he came to Leicester, but he worked as a factory worker when he first arrived, including a spell at Dunlop Tyres.

In Leicester, Avtar was instrumental in setting up youth groups, teaching folk dance, encouraging local poets and writers, and inspiring Communist activists. He gave up full-time employment in 1977 to study Youth and Community Work at Leicester University, and then gained an MA in Sociology at Warwick University. He became an employment officer and later a senior executive officer of the Race Equality Council.

Avtar was frequently seen on progressive platforms, always fighting for democracy, socialism and equality. He was a strong defender of the revolution in Cuba, and he supported the liberation struggles in South Africa, Palestine and Vietnam.

He had always been dedicated to socialism and Marxism, and was an active member of the Communist Party of India. When the CPI split in 1964, one faction broke away to form the CPI (Marxist), and the split in India was echoed in the UK. Avtar and the Leicester branch of the IWA, along with many other Midlands branches, became allied with the new CPI(M). The CPI(M) had many supporters in the Sikh community, although some Sikhs were unhappy when the CPI(M) opposed the demand for an independent Sikh state.

Avtar's first pen name was Avtar Singh Komal, but he later changed it to Avtar Sadiq to personify his dedication to secular democracy and socialist ideology. He wrote many poems and stories in Punjabi, but also wrote articles for the English press.

He joined the Leicester branch of the IWA in 1965, and was elected its cultural secretary. He became the secretary of the local writers' unit the following year. He was the founder of the Progressive Writers' Association in 1968. Hardev Dosanjh, a veteran member of the IWA, stated that "Sadiq's poetry symbolised the struggles of the working class for freedom, a world free of exploitation, with social and economic equality and a yearning for the alternative to neoliberalism — socialism."

Although Avtar Sadiq was of Sikh background and always wore his turban with pride, he believed that a person's religious beliefs were a private matter and should never be used for political purposes.

Avtar attended many events and meetings of Left parties in Europe and beyond. In 1994, he travelled to Cuba to participate in the first conference of the Cuban Institute of Friendship (ICAP), along with six other UK comrades. The delegation was led by Harkishan Singh Surjit, General Secretary of the CPI(M), who had organised a ship full of wheat and rice (10,000 tons) for the Cuban people. Avtar was delighted to meet Fidel Castro, the Cuban leader, on this visit.

Avtar went to Cuba again in 2002 for the second ICAP conference, this time with his friend Dyal Bagri and ten other UK comrades. This conference was attended by over four thousand delegates from 118 countries. Avtar wrote a book in Punjabi about this conference, the title of which translates as "Cuba — A Beacon of Struggle."

In the 2010 general election, Avtar Sadiq stood in Leicester East against the Labour candidate Keith Vaz, who had been the sitting MP there for twenty-three years. Avtar stood on behalf of the Unity for

Peace and Socialism, with the backing of the Communist Party of Britain (CPB).

In an interview with the *Morning Star*, he stated, "Whichever party wins the general election, there will be a need to project a socialist alternative to the neoliberal agenda favoured by all three of the major parties. By standing, I am representing those fighting back against the crisis, against war, against cuts to the welfare system, against racism and fascism. I stand shoulder to shoulder alongside CPB candidates, and with other Left forces standing in the election. It's not a matter of winning or losing, but of raising resistance and marching forward to build unity of all those trade union, labour and progressive forces."

In 2009, Avtar was a local candidate in the EU election, standing on the No2EU platform, initiated by the legendary Bob Crow, leader of the Rail, Maritime and Transport Workers (RMT) union.

Avtar was attending an international gathering of eminent Punjabi academics at a conference in India in November 2017, when he was taken ill. Despite this, he managed to deliver his address before returning to Leicester. His health deteriorated further and he died of heart failure in January 2018, leaving a wife, Gurdarshan Kaur and a son, Arvinder Kandola.

His Leicester IWA comrade, Dyal Bagri, tells me that Avtar was an excellent orator, especially on anti-imperialism, "He was a very good-natured and sociable person. It was a pleasure to work with him." Dyal also mentioned Avtar's love of cricket, football and other sports.

His long-time comrade, Mohinder Farma stated, "He was a remarkable role model for his peers and the next generation in impeccable socialist behaviour." IWA vice-president Harsev Baines commented that Avtar was equally comfortable organising a dance group or attending international conferences, adding, "Rest in peace, comrade, for you have truly earned it."

His widow told his friends, "Let there be no tears. Let us remember how he was always smiling and happy, never giving in to pain." Perhaps the final tribute should be that of his son. Arvinder said, "Dad always said that in life you should strive to improve yourself and serve others. Life is beautiful. It's given to you once, and should be lived with enjoyment and no regrets."

12. Hannah Mitchell: a radical career based on two weeks' schooling

Hannah Webster (1871–1956) was born in rural poverty in Alport Dale, in the remote Peak District of northwest Derbyshire, the daughter of a small farmer. She was the fourth of six children, and the middle one of three girls. Her father, John, was a kind and gentle man, but her mother possessed a violent temper. She had strong views about the duties of her three daughters, believing that their sole purpose in life was housework — cleaning and cooking. Hannah's sisters accepted their role, but Hannah resisted.

Her father and her uncle had taught Hannah to read and write, and she loved books. One particular favourite was the collected poems of William Wordsworth, left behind on a "permanent loan" by a visitor. She also managed to borrow copies of Elizabeth Gaskell's *Cranford* and Scott's *Kenilworth* from friendly neighbours.

Because the farm was so isolated, the nearest school was five miles away via a difficult track over the hills, which meant that to attend, the children would have to lodge in the school house during the week, returning home for weekends. Hannah's mother decreed that only one child at a time could attend school. Most of them managed to get two years of schooling, but when it came to Hannah's turn, she was only allowed two weeks, before being replaced by her younger sister. This meant that Hannah only had a fortnight's formal education during her entire childhood! Her mother obviously didn't want Hannah's love of reading to be encouraged. In her mother's philosophy, reading was a pastime for idlers who would be better employed scrubbing floors, churning butter and washing clothes. Hannah was expected to spend all her time working on the farm and on housework.

When mother flew into a rage, she sometimes drove the children out of the house, forcing them to sleep in the barn. She frequently hit them with a wooden stick or any other implement that came to hand. At the age of fourteen, after receiving a savage beating, Hannah seized the stick and threw it on the fire. After a word with her father, she fled the family home and walked seven miles across the moors to Glossop, where her married oldest brother was now living.

She found work in Glossop as a live-in maid in the house of a schoolmaster, his wife and four children. Although she had exchanged the domestic slavery at home for the drudgery of domestic service elsewhere, she did appreciate being able to read the books belonging to the household. What she did not appreciate quite so much was her low wage — four shillings a week — and being allowed off duty for only one evening per fortnight.

Two years later, much to the annoyance of her employer's wife, Hannah left domestic service to become a dressmaker's assistant at a shop in the town, at a wage double that of her previous job. She returned to live with her brother, now able to pay him a rent of two shillings per week. She spent the little money she had left after buying food on joining a lending library, and continued her education by reading avidly. She was very happy in her new position and enjoyed the company of her four colleagues in the dressmaking department.

However the position was only a temporary one for the summer months, and by autumn she was out of work. She moved to Bolton, Lancashire, to take up a post as an assistant in the clothing department of a shop, making and altering frocks. In Bolton, Hannah became interested in the campaign to give shop workers the right to a half day a week off, and she began to attend socialist meetings.

There she met Gibbon Mitchell, a young socialist who was working as a tailor's cutter. The couple became active supporters of the trade union movement, and they began to go to meetings of the Independent Labour Party. They married in 1895, and had a son, Frank. Because of her reluctance to bring more children into poverty, Hannah resolved to have no more. She and her husband agreed to use birth control, and had no further children.

Although Gibbon was a keen socialist, Hannah discovered that he found it hard to live up to her idea that they should share all the domestic chores. She was later to write, "Even the most sympathetic of men can never be made to understand that meals have to be planned, bought and cooked, and do not simply come up through the tablecloth." She says that she gradually became aware that male socialists are not necessarily feminists.

In 1897, they moved to Newhall, a mining village near Swadlincote in south Derbyshire, where Gibbon had taken a post with a firm of drapers. There they were able to rent a house with a garden at five shillings a week, and they began to keep poultry and grow vegetables. They quickly made contact with a group of socialists who had formed a local branch of the ILP. They also became involved with a group called the Brotherhood of Man, which had taken over a local pit to run it on co-operative principles. It was not long before a number of Welsh miners — driven out after a bitter strike in the mines of South Wales — arrived to work at the Brotherhood colliery. Hannah and Gibbon took one of the Welsh miners, together with his wife and child, into their home.

Hannah and Gibbon had long been avid readers of the weekly socialist newspaper, *The Clarion*. While they were in south Derbyshire, they very much enjoyed the visits of the *Clarion* van, which toured the country in the summer months, bringing socialist speakers to spread the word. The speakers would either sleep in the van, or stay with local socialists like the Mitchells. Hannah recalled the wonderful occasions when dozens of socialists from nearby villages, plus people from the towns of Burton and Lichfield, would cycle over to Newhall to listen to the *Clarion* speakers. Most supporters would bring their own food, but Hannah and Gibbon would sometimes feed members of the audience, thus leaving themselves short for the next week.

The Mitchells loved their three years in Newhall, but Gibbon was keen to find a job with the Co-op, and they returned to Lancashire when he got a job in the tailoring department of the Co-op in Ashton-under-Lyne. In March 1994, a plaque paying tribute to Hannah's life and work was attached to the wall of 43 Elizabeth Street, to mark the fact that she and Gibbon lived there for ten years.

Once in Ashton-under-Lyne, the Mitchells quickly became involved with the local ILP branch. Gibbon was made lecture secretary, a post that Hannah held later, and they entertained many speakers, including Keir Hardy, Philip Snowden and Victor Grayson. Gradually Hannah found she was called on to chair the meetings, and she also became a regular speaker herself.

In 1904, there was a vacancy on the Ashton Board of Guardians — they ran the local workhouse — and the ILP persuaded Hannah to stand. She was elected unopposed, but when she supported the practice of allowing the workhouse inmates beer with their Christmas lunch, she upset members of the local temperance movement, who ran a candidate against her when she was up for re-election.

Hannah was becoming interested in the women's suffrage movement and in 1904, along with many members of the ILP, she joined the Women's Social & Political Union, the organization later generally referred to as the suffragette movement. She wrote later that, "All my previous life had been a preparation for this great experience."

She visited the Pankhursts at their Manchester home, and became a frequent speaker on their platforms. Perhaps to make up for his shortcomings on the domestic front, Hannah's husband fully supported her when she joined the WSPU. There was a great deal of public hostility towards the suffragettes, and some of it became violent. From time to time, Gibbon — together with other ILP members — was called upon to become a steward at their public meetings, to deter physical attacks. Nevertheless the women were often threatened and physically attacked, particularly when they demonstrated in the open air, and when they heckled at Liberal Party meetings.

Often the attacks on the suffragettes were witnessed by police officers, who stood by and did nothing. On the false evidence of one policeman, Hannah was taken to court and found guilty of obstruction. When she refused to pay the fine imposed, she was sentenced to three days in prison. She was extremely annoyed on the second day to find she was to be released, Gibbon having paid her fine.

Hannah was an enthusiastic and committed member of the WSPU and became a paid part-time worker for the organization a year later. However, she did object to the high-handed way that the leaders of the WSPU, particularly Emmeline and Christabel Pankhurst, took major decisions without consulting the membership. This came to a head in 1907 when Emmeline Pankhurst announced that the WSPU's annual conference was cancelled and that future decisions would be taken by a committee which she would appoint.

Hannah Mitchell was persuaded by her friend Charlotte Despard to become a founder member of the breakaway Women's Freedom League, created by seventy members of the WSPU. The new organization grew to over 4,000 members and published its own newspaper, *The Voice*. Unlike the WSPU, the Women's Freedom League members continued to proclaim their pacifism during the 1914–18 war, and Hannah joined the No-Conscription Fellowship and the Women's Peace Council.

She became a well-known figure in public life, and in 1924 was elected as a member of Manchester City Council. The ILP had nominated her as a candidate in 1921 and 1923, but the Labour Party — to which the ILP was affiliated — was not willing to back a strong feminist woman with a mind of her own. However, they grudgingly accepted her nomination in 1924, and she was elected with a majority of eight votes. She was somewhat amused by the eagerness and desperation shown by some councillors to become the chair of a committee. Hannah was also startled to meet a fellow-member of the Libraries Committee who had never read a book.

By 1932, the ILP had disaffiliated from the Labour Party, but the Labour Party decided not to run a candidate against her. This was a wise move, given Hannah's reputation and popularity in her ward, and she was re-elected with a majority of over a thousand.

Hannah took an interest in the work of the local courts — she was a regular visitor there on behalf of the Women's Co-operative Guild — and in 1926 she became a magistrate, a Justice of the Peace. She enjoyed her JP work, and her humanity and understanding of the conditions of working women enabled her to play a vital part on the bench. She also said that her knowledge of ordinary people meant she could see through the occasional person who was "trying it on". She found that once the male magistrates got used to having women as colleagues, they were glad of their presence on the bench, and were generous enough to say so. Hannah Mitchell served as a JP for twenty years.

Hannah, a great lover of reading, had always had an ambition to write. Her earliest work was in the form of dialect sketches about current affairs, published in the ILP paper *The Northern Voice*, followed by articles on women in civic life published in a local newspaper. After successes in literary competitions, she began to write articles for the *Manchester Evening News*, including one on "Lovefeasts", calling on memories from her Derbyshire roots. Despite its name the Lovefeast was not a pagan orgy, but an annual Methodist get-together with eating of pies and cakes, beef and ham, combined with hymn-singing, personal testimonies, prayers and choruses. Every summer such a Lovefeast was held in the barn of Hannah's childhood farm, and she remembered it as one of the red-letter days of her year.

Following the publication of her article, Hannah was asked by local Methodists to turn it into a booklet. She did so, and was inordinately proud when she saw the published copies. She wrote, "I am sure that Dickens with all his fame never felt so proud as I did viewing that little pile of books bearing my name." Hannah felt that she had become a writer. Hannah also wrote the story of her life, but she kept it to herself and never saw it published. However it was edited by her grandson, Geoffrey Mitchell, and published posthumously by Virago in 1977, twenty-one years after Hannah's death, under the title *The Hard Way Up*. Virago described the book as "a unique record of a working-class woman's personal and political achievements."

In 2012 the Hannah Mitchell Foundation was formed as a forum for the development of devolved government in the north of England. The name was chosen "in memory of an outstanding Northern socialist, feminist and co-operator who was proud of her working class roots and had a cultural as well as political vision."

So Hannah Mitchell was a published writer, as well as a suffragette, a lifelong rebel, a magistrate, a city councillor, and a campaigner for women's rights, for workers' rights, and for peace. She was a much-admired figure in the public life of her adopted city — an amazing legacy for a woman with only two weeks' schooling.

13. Ida Hackett: "a lady of quality, a life-long socialist"

Ida Chrichlow was born on 11th December 1914, in Mansfield Woodhouse. Her dad was a miner, but he was blacklisted from Warsop Main colliery following the 1921 strike. He was unable to get employment for four years, but in 1925 he did manage to get a job at Bentley pit. He then transferred back to Warsop Main, just in time for the strike/lockout of 1926. The general strike was over in a week, but the miners carried on alone for thirty-two weeks. There was no dole for the strikers, but Ida's father managed to provide for his family by working five allotments, where he grew food, and by keeping fowls, and a pig which he co-owned with a neighbour. Meanwhile Ida's mother took in washing, and scrubbed floors for local shops. Ida had an early lesson in what being part of the organized working class was all about.

Ida left school at fourteen, and her first job was with the Co-op. She began as a pot washer, but quickly rose through the ranks — studying catering and book-keeping at night school — to become head waitress. In 1939, she was offered the job of manageress, but turned it down in order to marry local bricklayer Ernie Hackett. She was an active member of NUSDAW — the National Union of Shop, Distributive and Allied Workers — and from the beginning she attended its meetings. After each meeting she had to give a verbatim report to her father, a keen trade unionist. While she was still a lowly pot washer, she found that everything that was accidentally broken was taken from her wages, and, when washing pots all day, accidents were inevitable. One bad week she found that four shillings had been deducted from her five shillings pay. Ida decided to fight to get the system changed, and won a major concession, where just twopence a week was paid by all the workers to cover breakages. Another fight was over the uniforms. The girls had to provide their own, and Ida commented that whenever they bought new clothes for themselves, they were always brown so that they could end up being worn for work. Again Ida fought and won a clothing allowance.

Ida's parents were founder members of Mansfield Woodhouse Labour Party, and she joined the Labour League of Youth. She recalled leafleting for Charlie Brown in the 1929 general election. She thought he was a good MP, and quoted with approval that he opposed the National Government formed by Ramsay McDonald and the Conservatives. Up until the mid-1930s, Ida was convinced that if there was a strong Labour party and a strong Labour government, they would bring in the socialist changes that were needed. But she gradually became disillusioned with this approach and followed Ernie into the Communist Party, Ida joining in 1938, some three years after him. The Mansfield branch had about thirty-five members at the time, including Gerry Noble, the headmaster of Carter Lane School.

When war broke out in 1939, Ernie went into the Navy. Despite having a young baby, Ida became the full-time secretary of the CP branch. She did have the odd problem with the district secretary, who liked things done his own way. When Ida went down to see Ernie in Chatham one evening, to discuss the fact that he was training as a Petty Officer, her early morning train back to Mansfield was delayed by bad weather, and it was afternoon before she got into the office. The district secretary angrily asked where she'd been, and when she told him, he told Ida that she'd no right to go without discussing it with him. Deciding that she couldn't work with him, Ida took a job in the canteen of a small arms factory and joined the Transport and General Workers Union. Working in the canteen meant that she had contact with all the factory workers, and she set about recruiting them into the union. After a year, she'd got nineteen women collecting union subs and attending committee meetings.

When the war finished, there was the 1945 election. Ernie was still in the Navy, and when Ida wrote to him to say that she feared there would be a coalition government elected, Ernie replied that the armed forces wouldn't stand for that. He forecast — correctly — an overwhelming Labour victory. Ida commented, "That was our love letters during the war!"

After the war, Ida went into the hosiery industry. When she applied for a job at Foster, Clay and Ward in Newgate Lane, she was shown round by a Mr Brown. After the tour, he told her that she'd asked more questions than anybody he'd ever met. He then added a complaint that when he went round the factory the women carried on chattering and singing, whereas before the war, everyone would shut up when he came round. He felt that his position had been undermined. Ida said that she felt her hackles rising. "Mr Brown," she said. "My husband's just done five years fighting fascism and I'm not going to work for a little Hitler." She claims that she was sacked before she'd started.

She did get a job at a hosiery factory in Belverdere Street, but where she sat, there was a lavatory door next to her. The lavatory had a lot of people using it, and because it wasn't cleaned often enough, it smelled horrible. Ida went to see the deputy manager to ask what could be done about the unhygienic lavatory. When the man exploded with rage, she told him that she'd have to have a word when the inspectors came round from head office. Although she was in her first week there, she didn't get the sack this time, and the condition of the lavatory improved. It wasn't long before Ida had got the majority of the women to join the union, and she became shop steward.

The union meetings were held on Sunday mornings, but even there Ida met some misogyny. The union secretary looked aghast at Ida and asked her, "Who's cooking your husband's dinner?" When she replied that Ernest was because they always worked as a team, she was told, "Well, that wouldn't do for me!" She found that the union was only interested in the men's pay and conditions. The women were on their own, but they did have Ida to safeguard their interests.

When the women at the factory were asked to do some difficult work that meant that they would hardly be able to earn anything on the piecework rates, Ida went to see the manager to negotiate a better price on it. The result was that she was told to leave the premises. She'd been sacked. When she went to collect her belongings, she told the other women what had happened. The result was instantaneous — if Ida was going, everyone was going. They all — the menders, the seamers, the linkers — walked out of the factory.

Even when the workers were offered a better price for the work, they replied that they would not return to work without Ida Hackett. Eventually, she was taken back, but had to work in a small room on her own, and her work was subject to constant checking by a special "inspector." Although Ida was hardly earning enough to cover her bus fare, she gritted her teeth and tenaciously carried on, until the firm allowed her back into the main room with the other women.

Ida also continued with her Party work, becoming a member of the District Committee in 1946, and its chair in 1952. In 1954, she was selected to go, as a delegate from the National Assembly of Women, to the Soviet Union.

She became well known throughout the East Midlands for her willingness to support all progressive causes. If there was a fight, Ida Hackett was there at its heart. One example was when she and Ernest organized the tenants' campaign and rent strike against the Tory Housing Finance Act. On another occasion, she fought a local battle over concessionary bus tokens. These tokens could not be used until after 9.30am, meaning that anyone with a hospital or doctor's appointment earlier had to pay full fare. Ida thought that was not right — she campaigned and she won the day.

Sometimes, Ida's reputation as a fearless and doughty fighter went before her. She recalled an occasion when she joined the National Association of Old Age Pensioners, and turned up at a meeting in Mansfield. She was greeted by the somewhat self-important secretary, saying, "Why are you here? We don't want you — you cause trouble." However, the women in the audience intervened with a chorus of "Take no notice, Ida. You come and sit with us." Again her popularity with the ordinary people of the town had stood her in good stead.

Not surprisingly, Ida played a central role during the 1984–85 miners' strike. Most people know that in Nottinghamshire the majority of miners did not strike, they carried on working. What many do not realize is that a substantial number of Notts miners did come out on strike. Seven thousand miners went on strike, although that number did reduce by half as the strike went on. Every Nottinghamshire pit had miners out on strike, forming a picket, challenging those miners who chose to scab. Every pit had its women's support group: miners' wives, miners' daughters, miners' supporters, who raised funds, went on picket lines, cooked meals for the families of the striking miners, and raised the profile of the strikers.

Two of the women of the women's support group at Blidworth colliery — Pauline and Doreen — had their story immortalized in the excellent book *Shifting Horizons* by Lynn Beaton. The book is well-titled. Many women did have their horizons shifted by the strike. They became more self-aware, more politicised, some going on to become activists and organizers in other fields. Of course, Ida Hackett didn't need politicising — she was already there.

Although each of the twenty-seven pits had its own women's group, it was necessary to have a county-wide coordinating committee working across the whole coalfield. The Women Against Pit Closures Committee was formed and was chaired by the formidable Ida. Despite being seventy, and with a very ill husband — Ernie had suffered two strokes and three heart attacks — Ida threw herself into the campaign. When some foolish journalist asked her about running the "soup kitchens" Ida bristled and pointed out that "We didn't have soup kitchens. They were real food kitchens in village halls and schools, providing full meals for the families."

Ida ranked the women who worked with her to support the striking miners — including vicar's daughter Liz Hollis, the campaign group secretary — as being on a par with the suffragettes and the women of Greenham Common. When one NUM official commented that behind every striking miner there is a good woman, Ida put him right. "She's not behind him, she is alongside — or even in front!"

The strikers in Notts were receiving no funds from the local union, leaving them dependent on whatever could be raised. Each week, women from the individual pit support groups came to the central committee to collect money donated by the Union of Communication Workers in London. Help came in — money and goods — from all over the country, especially after Ida had written a letter, published in the *Morning Star*, asking for help. Ida then went to London herself to set up a network of support. Money was sent to Nottinghamshire from ASLEF (the train drivers' union) and other unions, and from individuals. A couple in Essex sent £5 with a note saying they were glad to see the women were part of the fight. One donation that touched Ida deeply was a bag of nuts sent from a peasant woman in India.

By November, £4000 a week was coming in, and this was used to support the families of the striking miners. Children were given pocket money and clothing, and in December 1984, Christmas parties were held. One supporter raised cash through a sponsored parachute jump. A firm of solicitors sent a donation. Ida knew how important it was for the strike that people shouldn't have their electricity or gas cut off, or their homes repossessed.

Despite her age, Ida was also there on the picket lines, and recalls being jostled and chased by the police. She found the police intimidating, but says that it was worse for those women with young children, worrying that they might be arrested. While Ida was busy raising funds and standing on the picket lines, Ernest worked from home, answering the phone, and writing letters. In July, Ida and Ernie attended a magnificent Food for Victory event held at the Forest recreation ground in Nottingham. There were eight thousand people there and Ida and Ernie were presented with a miners' lamp and a bouquet to mark their outstanding contribution to the struggle. It was also the day of their forty-fifth wedding anniversary.

When the strike ended in March 1985, Ida joined the campaign to reinstate the fourteen Nottinghamshire miners who had been sacked, and was involved in providing help for their families. Ernest Hackett died in 1985, a few weeks after the end of the strike, but Ida lived on in Mansfield, still supporting the struggle to improve the position of the ordinary working man and woman. She was still fighting for socialism, and still a CP member, up to her death on Monday 23 April 2012. She was ninety-eight years young.

Among the many tributes from people in politics and her own family and friends, her obituary in the *Morning Star* included the comment that "Ida dressed immaculately — blue rinse even — and her house was as smart as she". This reminder of a very human side of Ida is a useful indication that, should you have ever met a well-dressed and blue-rinsed lady in the Nottinghamshire area, it would have been a foolish error to assume she was a typical conservative!

14. Dennis Skinner: miner and socialist MP

Dennis Skinner is a hero to many of us but he also commands the grudging respect of people who do not share his socialist ideals. After I'd given a talk in Bolsover — and Dennis Skinner was mentioned in the talk — one member of the audience told me, "I have never voted Labour in my life, but I have to admit that Dennis Skinner never says one thing and does the opposite. If Dennis says he'll do something, he does it. He's an honest MP and that's a bloody rare creature."

Dennis can be seen and heard in his favourite seat in the House of Commons, just below the central gangway, making things difficult for anyone he thinks is being hypocritical or underhand. He was once forced by the Speaker to withdraw a comment about Mrs Thatcher telling a lie. Under Parliamentary convention, no MP is capable of telling lies! Dennis withdrew the word liar, but somehow managed to get away with saying "but she wouldn't recognise the truth if it was sprayed on her eyeballs."

Dennis is famous for his witty asides delivered in the familiar Derbyshire accent. No-one will ever forget the occasion when a Tory minister rose to speak with one hand casually tucked into his trouser pocket. From the direction of his customary seat, the whole house heard a loud query as to whether the minister was "playing with hisself." The embarrassed minister was unable to decide whether to quickly withdraw the offending hand, thus provoking the follow up "I was right!" from Dennis, or to continue with his hand in his pocket. I don't think he made that error again.

Dennis was born in Clay Cross in February 1932. He did well in his local primary school, and at the age of ten he was awarded a county scholarship, entitling him to attend Tupton Grammar School. This was not the eleven-plus system of the post-war years when something like 25% of children were awarded grammar school places. In 1942, there were just eighteen scholarships in the whole of Derbyshire and Dennis won one of them.

He did well and gained a good school certificate. However he decided not to stay on at school and go into the sixth form. At sixteen, he left school and went to work down the pit. "My parents weren't too happy about it, thinking it was a waste of my education," Dennis told me, "but I was aware that I was in danger of growing away from my mates. They had all gone down the pit at the age of fourteen."

The first pit where he worked was Parkhouse Colliery, a shallow pit and very cold. He explained that the deeper the pit, the warmer the temperature. His employers would have liked him to work towards becoming a manager, but for Dennis the pull of the Union was much stronger. He became the National Union of Mineworkers delegate for his colliery, and found that his education enabled him to negotiate successfully with the management. "I could think on my feet, and could calculate figures quicker than they could," he says.

When Parkhouse closed, he moved to the much larger Glapwell Colliery, and was soon voted in as vice-president of Derbyshire NUM, moving up to county president at the age of thirty-three. He was considering becoming a full-time union official but at this time he was asked to stand for election as a local councillor. "Labour lost control of Clay Cross Urban District Council," he explained, "and it was important to win it back." He stood, he was elected and Labour won back the council majority. His political life continued and he was elected onto Derbyshire County Council in 1966.

The local MP had expressed his intention to step down, and Dennis was asked to consider standing in the 1970 general election. He had to weigh up this change in his life against the possibility of full-time union work, but was persuaded to stand. He was successful and was elected to the House of Commons. He has been the member for the Bolsover constituency ever since, continuing to fight for full-blooded socialism.

When he arrived in Parliament, Dennis found himself a backbench MP, but in opposition. The Tories had won the election with a majority of thirty. Not long after he'd arrived at the House of Commons, there was a series of votes late into the night. At nearly midnight, a Conservative MP, keen to leave the Commons and be off socialising somewhere, approached Dennis and asked him if he had a pair. Dennis raised his eyebrows, and the man hastily explained that if the two of them formed a pair, this meant that they could both go home. Without actually agreeing to pair, Dennis did advise the man that he should go home. The grateful member hurried away, and the government majority fell by one.

A second Conservative approached him with the same request, and he too was dispatched. After a third one went home, Dennis was by now convinced that he'd cracked the system. He had managed to find a way to reduce the government's majority and would surely earn his Party's eternal gratitude.

It did not work out that way. It was the chief Labour whip who called Dennis to see him the next day. It was not to express his thanks, but to reprimand him for wrecking the system. It was all based on trust, he explained, and young Dennis Skinner was spoiling it. Dennis tells me that he did explain that he hadn't actually agreed to pair, but had simply advised the Tories to go home. The Labour whip, Bob Mellish, was not amused. Dennis, not for the last time, was in trouble with his own Party officials.

Pairing — agreeing with a member of another party to absent themselves from Parliament without affecting the government's majority — is one of the things that Dennis Skinner has never done in his nearly five decades as an MP.

He tells me that he has three self-imposed rules. One is never to go on foreign trips financed by anyone else. "If a firm or a foreign country is paying for the trip, they are going to want a payback in some way," he says.

His second abiding principle is never to drink in the House of Commons bar. "I'm not being puritanical," he states, "but the place is full of journalists listening in to conversations. If an MP has a drink and says something indiscreet, then it'll be in the media the next day." I also get the impression that Dennis believes that a miner being drunk at work would be sacked on the spot, so why should an MP's place of work be any different?

His third principle is to abstain from pairing. He feels that if he is being paid to be there in the House of Commons, he should not be absent.

As a young man, Dennis took part in cycling, football, athletics, road-walking, cricket and tennis. He had even taken part in marathons. Although he had smoked as a young man, he gave up over fifty years ago. It was, therefore, a shock when, in 1999, he discovered cancer: a tumour in his bladder. This was successfully removed, and he now only needs an annual check-up. Worse was to happen in 2003. While taking a "treadmill test," he collapsed and was found to be suffering from blocked arteries. He needed a heart bypass.

He was back at work within eight weeks, keen to get on with the job he was elected to do, to represent his Derbyshire constituents.

Despite being seventy-two at the time, he was keen to return to Parliament.

His fitness returned, and it was not long before he climbed up Kinder Scout, Derbyshire's highest peak, to scatter the ashes of his late brother Gordon. Dennis comes from a close Derbyshire family of seven brothers and two sisters. The whole family is deeply committed to socialist politics. Two of his brothers were members of the Clay Cross council, which was "fined" under Margaret Thatcher for refusing to put up the rents of council tenants. One family friend told me that Dennis — regarded by the media as being on the hard left — is the most moderate member of the Skinner clan.

Dennis once had to compete for his accustomed location in the House of Commons with David Owen, then leader of the SDP, who had started to leave his prayer card to reserve that seat. Dennis even tried attending prayers himself to get his own card in place, but Owen's card was getting there earlier and earlier. When Dennis found out that David Owen wasn't actually putting it there himself, but was — against all the rules — sending a researcher from his office to do so, he was understandably annoyed. It's never a good idea to take on an ex-miner from Derbyshire, especially if he's one of the Skinner clan. It wasn't long before Dennis was back in his old place with his comrades Bob Cryer, Dennis Canavan and Ioan Evans!

The mutual dislike between Dennis Skinner and David Owen continued. While raising a point of order, Dennis refered to his old enemy as "a pompous sod." The Speaker, Bernard Weatherall, ordered him to withdraw the comment. Dennis replied that since he was feeling in a good mood, he was prepared to withdraw the word "pompous." As that wasn't the word that the Speaker wanted withdrawn, and Dennis was adamant, he was kicked out of the Chamber for the day.

I once heard a very timid newly-elected MP complain tearfully that his Party whip was bullying him, holding him by his jacket lapels and threatening him with physical violence if he didn't vote the way he was told. I cannot imagine any whip, however large and well-built, had ever dreamed of using that tactic on the Beast of Bolsover!

Dennis was able to use his experience of how things are done — and where and when to exert pressure — to enable a business park to be built on the site of two former collieries, Markham and Shirebrook, to provide employment for the families of his constituents, many of the former miners. He also suggested that a spur should be built between junctions

29 and 30 of the M1 motorway. "They all said the idea of a new motorway junction was mad," he said, "but the money was found." There is now a junction 29a on the M1. Never tell Dennis Skinner that an idea is impossible.

While the Beast of Bolsover can continue to achieve such things for his people, I reckon he will continue as a truthful and brutally honest politician. Dennis Skinner is a legend in his own lifetime.

15. A cathedral of unbelief and a socialist church

Two places in Leicester of great interest to people on the left are Secular Hall on Humberstone Gate and the former St Mark's Church on Belgrave Road.

Secular Hall was opened in 1881 as a meeting place for local humanists and freethinkers, after they had been denied permission by Thomas Cooke, a strong Baptist, to use the city's Temperance Hall. Secularists were frequently refused the use of public meeting rooms, either because they were owned by religious bodies, or because the church put pressure on pub landlords. George Jacob Holyoake was refused use of a public room at the Three Crowns for a secular talk in 1869.

The money for the building of Secular Hall was provided by the family of Josiah Gimson, the renowned Leicester engineer, and businessman Michael Wright. The architect was W. Larner Sugden of Leek. It was not long before the new hall was termed by one critic "a cathedral of unbelief."

Above the entrance are three panels with symbols depicting Liberty, Justice and Truth. Below these are terracotta busts, created by Ambrose

Louis Vago, of five philosophers: Socrates, Voltaire, Tom Paine, Robert Owen and Jesus. If the inclusion of Jesus was intended to smooth the ruffled feathers of local churchgoers, it had the opposite effect. The idea of giving equal importance to Jesus and Tom Paine caused outrage, and a certain Canon Vaughan demanded — unsuccessfully — that the bust of Jesus be removed.

Josiah Gimson and Michael Wright died soon after the opening of the Hall, but Sydney Gimson, son of Josiah, remained President of the Society until 1938. The ownership of the hall was transferred to Leicester Rationalist Trust in 1907.

William Morris came to lecture on Art and Socialism, staying at the home of Sydney and Ernest Gimson, and Annie Besant, George Bernard Shaw, Charles Bradlaugh, Peter Kropotkin, Emma Goldman and Bertrand Russell were also guests who came to speak here.

Secular Hall is still in regular use. At one time, such halls for freethinkers were widespread, but today Secular Hall in Leicester is the only one in the country outside London. Leicester Secular Hall is a Grade II listed building and it is the only Secular Hall still used by a secular society. Leicester Secular Society lectures and meetings are still held there.

* * *

A somewhat different and unusual monument in Leicester is to be found in the former St Mark's Church in Belgrave Road. It dates from a time when the vicar at St Mark's was Frederick Lewis Donaldson. Donaldson (1860–1953) was a committed Christian socialist, and stated that "Christianity is the religion of which socialism is the practice." He wrote that socialism was a "glorious principle of organic growth showing development from lower to higher conditions of life and organization."

After a year as vicar of the mining village of Nailstone in North West Leicestershire, he came to Leicester in 1896. In a pamphlet he wrote, "St. Mark's is one of the chief working-class parishes of the town, and contains towards 15,000 souls. In this parish there is represented much of the tragedy and pathos, shame and horror of modern social conditions — infant mortality, child labour, underpayment or sweating of men and women, decadence of physical life, consumption and premature death."

Lewis Donaldson was an active campaigner for socialism. He was one of the founder members of the Church Socialist League, and for ten years he was chairman of the local branch of the Christian Social Union.

One of his main concerns was with the unemployed of Leicester, and he was one of the leaders of the march of unemployed shoemakers to

London in June 1905. After a mass meeting in Leicester, attended by a quarter of the population of the city, he accompanied them all the way as their chaplain. Before the march, he had written to the Archbishop of Canterbury, Randall Davidson, asking him to meet with the unemployed marchers at Lambeth. The Archbishop refused. The correspondence between Lewis Donaldson and the Archbishop was later published, and it has been said that this cost Donaldson a future post as a bishop himself.

Donaldson was also a supporter of women's suffrage and, in 1913, he led a deputation of clergymen to the prime minister, Herbert Asquith, to demand that women be given the vote.

A physical reminder of the Leicester socialist cleric and his beliefs can still be seen in the former St Mark's Church building. In 1910, Lewis Donaldson commissioned James Eadie-Reid of Gateshead, to paint seven murals depicting Christ as the Apotheosis of Labour. Reid (1856–1926) had studied in Edinburgh and was a friend and admirer of the Pre-Raphaelite Brotherhood. He specialised in stained-glass windows and murals.

Donaldson himself supervised the painting of seven large canvas panels painted in oils.

One of the outer panels shows the misery of working people in the Edwardian era. It shows an old man with bowed head, worn out by a

lifetime of physical labour. Next to him is the figure of a twelve-year-old girl, forced to leave her education to work in a factory, and a bandaged man, suffering from injuries incurred in an industrial accident. A fourth figure, head in hands, is that of an unemployed worker.

One panel shows workers, heavy-laden and oppressed, unable to look up, while above them is Mammon, driving past in his car and accompanied by Luxury, an elegant silk-clad woman. Behind them are clouds of pollution coming from the factories. Above them all the Angel of Pity looks down.

Other panels show a more hopeful scene: a socialist society where the dignity of work is respected, where talent is encouraged, through education and the arts. One panel shows a musician, a painter, a stonemason and an architect, together with a mother and child, representing the flourishing of the creative arts, together with six of the apostles, themselves working men of their day.

Another panel shows progress through cooperation. On it a miner, a factory worker and a farmer, together with a man and woman hand in hand, show how cooperation and socialism can lead to a better world, free of the capitalism and competition that divide people. The man and woman walking together indicate that Donaldson believed in the rights of women, as well as the rights of men.

A nearby window, also designed for Donaldson by James Eadie-Reid, is entitled "History in the Record of Man's Struggle to be Free". It is actually a war memorial, but it is looking forward to a New Jerusalem. Among the characters depicted are an African — Donaldson's vision was worldwide. A Free Church minister and a Catholic priest work together in the cause — very ecumenical — and a woman breaks free of her chains. Another figure holds the charter of the League of Nations.

St Mark's Church closed in 1986, and stood empty for almost twenty years. The Grade II* Listed Building is now a banqueting hall and the socialist murals are still on display, though reports indicate that they may be fading. It seems to me ironic that this building, given its socialist history, is now called The Empire.

16. Walter Gregory: volunteer with the International Brigades

Walter was born in Lincoln in 1913, his parents having moved there from Newark just before his birth. Walter left school at the age of fourteen and found a clerical post. He supplemented his wages by taking a second job, delivering prescriptions for the local doctor. He attended night school three times a week, studying bookkeeping, English and shorthand. He became the main family breadwinner when his dad died in 1930, but was made redundant in 1932. He would have taken any job, clerical or manual, but was unable to find work. He started to take an interest in politics and joined the Labour League of Youth. He also began to attend classes run by the WEA, studying politics and economics.

Walter joined the No More War Movement, and met men who had been conscientious objectors during WWI. He admired these men and their courage, but his commitment to pacifism began to come into conflict with what he was learning about the growing strength of fascism. He joined the National Unemployed Workers' Movement and when he heard that the Tyneside contingent of the NUWM was to pass through Lincoln on its hunger march to London, Walter decided to join them.

Soon after this, the Gregory family returned to its Nottinghamshire roots, moving to Bulwell. He soon joined the local branch of the NUWM, and also the Communist Party. Desperate for work, he actually joined the army in 1934, and at Aldershot he learned to maintain and use a rifle. However, his army career was short-lived as — rather to his embarrassment — he failed the clerical exam. This seems surprising, and I wonder if his practice of reading out bits from the *Daily Worker* in the barrack-room was the true reason he was failed.

A branch of the British Union of Fascists had been established in Nottingham, and Walter sustained his first wound in his lifelong fight against fascism when Oswald Mosley came to Victoria Baths to address a meeting. Walter and several comrades managed to get into the meeting, and when the fascist leader — posing theatrically under a single spotlight against a black background — began to declaim his message, they began to heckle. Walter was hit over the head with a chair, and had his nose broken.

Despite this early injury, Walter continued to attend and heckle fascist meetings, including one at West Bridgford, addressed by a little-known fascist called William Joyce — later to become infamous as Lord Haw Haw, notorious for his wartime broadcasts from Hitler's Germany.

In 1936, Walter Gregory was approached by the Communist Party organiser for Nottingham, who asked if he would like to volunteer to fight with the International Brigades in Spain. All volunteers had to be over twenty-one and unmarried, and Walter qualified on both counts. Walter's immediate response was, "Yes, I'll go. How do I get there?"

The Spanish Civil War had begun after a declaration of opposition by a group of generals — one was Franco — against the elected Government of the Second Spanish Republic. The military coup was supported by the fascists, the monarchists, and the Catholic church. The generals also received the support of Nazi Germany and fascist Italy. Many countries, including Britain, adopted a neutral non-interventionist policy, but across the world democratically-minded people wanted to help the ordinary people of Spain fight the military coup. Although forbidden by the British government, over two thousand men went from Britain to Spain to fight for the elected Republican government. It was not only CP members who went: about half of the volunteers were members of other political organizations or members of no party at all. A quarter of the volunteers were to die in the fighting.

Despite having no passport, Walter travelled to London by train, then on the midnight boat to Dunkirk, pretending he was on a day trip. He made his way to Paris and then via Marseilles to Perpignon. From Perpignon, he and the other volunteers were taken by bus across the border into Spain. In Figueras, they were billeted in the dungeons of a local castle before moving on to Barcelona, where they received a fantastic reception.

Walter describes the city as an awe-inspiring spectacle of enthusiasm and noise. It was a city in the full flood of revolutionary zest and zeal. Every building was flying the red flag of the communists, the red and black flags of the anarchists, or the colours of the Catalan nationalists.

Eventually he reached Albacete, the centre for the International Brigades. The six hundred volunteers assembled in the town's bull ring and paraded in their national groups: French, German, and British. The British contingent was taken on to Madrigueras, where they were issued with rifles, boots, khaki uniforms, tin hats and two coarse woollen blankets. The Battalon Ingles was officially entitled XVI Battalion, XV Brigade of the 35th Division of the Spanish Republican Army, but was commonly called the British Battalion. It comprised three infantry companies of a hundred men plus a machine gun company, each company under the command of a military lieutenant and a political commissar. Walter was made *enlace* or messenger to his lieutenant, Bill Briskey, and because they had no radios or telephones, he covered many miles on foot carrying messages, frequently under enemy fire.

Although the food was poor and water was in short supply, the men were pleased to find that the local wine was plentiful and cheap. Walter was pleasantly surprised to learn that as a volunteer he was to be paid five pesetas a day.

After five weeks of training, they were ready for battle. Walter's first time in action was at the battle of Jarama. The fascist forces — professional soldiers — were equipped with German and Italian tanks. The generals' coup had begun in Morocco, from where they seized the southern cities of Cádiz, Granada, Seville and Córdoba.

The fascists were determined to capture Madrid, but their attempts to push in from the west were met with fierce resistance from the people of the city. The terrain north of the capital was not suitable for the fascists' tanks and heavy artillery so they swung south. By January 1937, 40,000 fascist troops were ready for an assault across the valley of the River Jarama in order to cut off the Madrid/Valencia road.

In this battle, Walter, still acting as the *enlace* for Bill Briskey, was shot in the knuckle of his thumb, and ended up with it somewhat shortened and unable to bend. He also saw Bill shot dead as he ran towards Walter. It appears that a sniper had Walter in his sights, but switched from the messenger to the officer at the last second.

The song "Jarama Valley" was written by Alex McDade, a member of the British Battalion. Alex, a Glaswegian, was the political commissar of the Brigade and therefore responsible for the men's welfare.

There are several versions of the song, some adapting the British battalion to Lincoln Battalion and thus remembering the part paid by American volunteers in the battle. The song was adapted and recorded by Woody Guthrie, and later by Pete Seeger.

One version begins:

> There's a valley in Spain called Jarama
> It's a place the we all know so well,
> It is there that we gave of our manhood,
> And so many of our brave comrades fell.

We are proud of the British Battalion,
And the stand for Madrid that they made,
For they fought like true sons of the soil,
As part of the Fifteenth Brigade.

With the rest of the international column,
In the stand for the freedom of Spain,
We swore in the valley of Jarama
That fascism never will reign.

After three months in hospital, Walter returned to action. The battle of Jarama — in which Walter had been involved for only one day — had been a defensive one, and the Republicans had succeeded in keeping the fascist troops from crossing the valley, though at a terrible cost in terms of lives. The British Battalion lost 225 of its 600 men, and the Lincoln Battalion 125 out of 500.

His second experience of action came when the Republicans attacked a fortified village called Villanueva de la Cañada. Like all Spanish villages the highest building was a church, and as the British brigade grew closer, they were met by a terrifying onslaught of machine-gun fire from the top of the church. Walter and his good friend Taff leapt into a ditch. Throughout the march, Taff had been telling Walter about a wonderful Welsh pub and Walter had decided that after the war, he and Taff would have a beer there. In the comparative safety of the ditch, Walter turned to speak to Taff, only to find him shot dead with a bullet through his forehead. Walter also discovered that he had been hit himself, a machine gun bullet having passed clean through his arm. He put on a temporary dressing and carried on with the battle.

What he experienced next haunted him for the rest of his life. A group of women and children were leaving the village and coming towards the soldiers of the British Brigade. They shouted to them, telling them to hurry up and get to safety, when they saw to their horror that they were being used as a human shield by a group of fascist soldiers who were forcing the group forward at bayonet point. The fascists began to shoot at Walter and his comrades, and a number of the women and children were injured in the encounter.

By nightfall, Walter's injured arm forced him to seek treatment and he managed to get to the hospital in Madrid. There, Walter noticed members of the women's militia fighting on the front line, something he hadn't come across elsewhere. He admits that he and others of the walking wounded did make a hazardous journey to a bar in the area under fire when they heard a rumour that it had received a consignment of beer. The trip was extremely perilous and he vowed not to repeat the escapade.

Walter returned to active combat and fought at Brunete, where the battalion took such a hammering that 550 of the 600 men were wounded or dead. The dead included Alex McDade. The survivors were exhausted, and suffering from heat, hunger and thirst. They were at a low ebb. It looked as if the fascists had won, but General Franco suddenly decided to leave the siege of Madrid to concentrate on attacking the Republican stronghold on the north coast of Spain. Within three weeks the battalion numbers were up to full strength, boosted by new recruits and men recovering from their injuries.

Later Walter fought in the battle of Purburrell Hill, where they were attacking a fascist stronghold defended with machine gun emplacements. Despite suffering many fatalities on the first day, the British Battalion managed to take the hill. Combining with the Lincoln Battalion they fought their way into Belchite, fighting street by street with grenades and petrol bombs, in what Walter says was the bloodiest fighting he had yet seen, with no quarter given by either side. On 6th September, the fascists surrendered leaving both Quinto and Belchite in Republican hands. Throughout all the fighting, Walter was — as *enlace* — still running across exposed lands to carry messages between units.

After less than a year of fighting, Walter was becoming a comparative veteran, given the rate of casualties. However, he was amazed to be told that he was to undergo officer training. He had always thought of himself as a rank and file volunteer soldier. The training took place at Tarazona in an area controlled by the anarchists, whom Walter came to admire very much for their tenacity and enthusiasm, their sincerity and courage. The only complaint he had was that he couldn't celebrate Christmas in any way, the anarchists being fiercely anti-clerical. He was trained in battle tactics, and how to strip, assemble and fire a machine gun in the dark. He passed the course and was now an acting lieutenant, known as Teniente Gregorio.

His first job was to train new recruits, a few of them British but the majority Spanish. Although he enjoyed this, he felt that he should be on the front line, not in the relative safety of the training school, especially when he heard of the death in battle of Bernard Winfield, a friend from Nottingham. In February 1938 he was allowed to rejoin his comrades in Lécera, taking with him 200 of his recruits. By this time, about half of the British battalion were in fact Spaniards, a situation Walter welcomed since he had always been puzzled by the practice of having national battalions.

In March 1938, Franco launched a massive assault, using concentrations of tanks to create breaks in the Republican defences, followed by air raids and artillery attacks. The British battalion was to defend the town of Belchite, but was facing forces of far greater numbers and more powerful weapons. In face of the fascist onslaught they were forced to retreat. The International Brigades suffered terrible casualties and there were only 200 men left — British, American, Canadian, German and Spanish — as they retreated along the Gandesa-Tortosa road. At one point the road ran through a cutting flanked by a steep ridge. This was an ideal terrain to temporarily hold the road against the pursuing fascists. Walter with twelve volunteers under his command, climbed the steep slope and established a position.

Walter and his comrades held this position, while the rest of the soldiers continued along the road, fending off first a cavalry patrol, and then preventing the main enemy troops from entering the pass. They held their position until midnight, then slipped away to catch up with the rest of volunteers as they queued to cross the River Ebro. Once across, the bridge was destroyed to prevent the fascists from following.

Walter lost many close friends at this stage of the war. One he particularly mourned was Wally Tapsell, a cockney described by Walter as "the greatest of all those who served as political commissars." He last saw him firing at the oncoming enemy tanks before being hit, and says he hopes Wally was killed in action, rather than wounded and captured, since the fascists would have tortured and executed him.

It was now April 1938. After twenty-one months of war, the Republic was on the verge of collapse. Strafed by German planes, and bombarded by the fascists' fast-moving columns of tanks, the Republican army retreated into Catalonia. The Republic was now split into two: Catalonia and a large enclave in south-east Spain.

Despite the odds stacked against it, the Republic managed to fight on valiantly for another year. They had two strokes of luck. One was that Franco decided to strike south towards Valencia, rather than cross the Ebro towards Catalonia. The other was that France now had a socialist president, Leon Blum, who opened the border, enabling supplies of food and arms to travel through France into Catalonia.

The Republicans in Catalonia had three months to regroup and rearm. It was decided that attack was the best form of defence, and on 23 July, the XVth Brigade took part in a night-time crossing of the fast-flowing River Ebro. If they had crossed in daylight, they would have been strafed by fascist planes and shelled by tanks. Walter and his comrades advanced westwards, but when dawn broke, the fascist air force detected them and began to strafe.

Walter and his unit managed to rush and capture a hill where Nationalist machine guns were in place. However, when they attempted to take Hill 481, nicknamed the Pimple, they were less successful.

Later Walter took a bullet wound in the neck, fired by a sniper. His comment is amazing. "I have to credit my assailant with superb shooting. He fired just once and he hit me. Beautiful shooting, but luckily for me, not quite good enough." The walking wounded and others on stretchers had to make their way back to the river. There, under heavy fire, Walter managed to cross what was left of the pontoon. He was transported by lorry and train to Barcelona, then north to a hospital in Mataró, where he found himself in a bed next to Jack Jones, who later became a trade union leader. Walter's wound was not serious, and a few days later he was back in action.

However, things were now dire. The depleted front-line Republican brigades were now facing 100,000 fascist troops with massive artillery support, and the British brigade suffered heavy casualties. Despite fighting valiantly, they were continuously bombed. Walter found himself with just two dozen men left, and was eventually taken prisoner. He managed to discard his jacket. Had the fascists realized he was a Teniente and a veteran of the war, he would have been tortured and inevitably executed by firing squad. Like all his fellow prisoners, he claimed to be a newly-arrived volunteer.

Ironically, Walter's capture came on the last day of fighting for the International Brigades. In a speech to the League of Nations, the president of the Republic, Juan Negrín, offered to withdraw the International Brigades from Spain under the supervision of observers appointed by the League.

As the International Brigades assembled in Barcelona for their farewell parade, they were addressed by the Republican heroine, Dolores Ibárruri — always known as La Pasionara. She told the departing volunteers, "You can go with pride. You are history. You are legend. You are the heroic example of the solidarity and the universality of democracy. We will not forget you."

Walter and the other captured comrades, however, were still prisoners of the fascists. He was subjected to repeated interrogations by the Nationalist officers. He cell was completely unfurnished, the bed, table and chair having been removed. There was no bedding, so he had to sleep crouched with his back to the wall. The crucifix high up on the wall had the usual figure of Christ, but wearing a loin cloth in the yellow and red stripes of Franco's fascist movement.

After being interrogated by a panel of top fascist officers in immaculate tailored uniforms, he heard one of them say, "Yes, he is English," and he was returned to his cell. At dusk a few days later, a two-man escort took him from his cell. Walter was convinced he was to be shot, since that had been the fate of others who had been interviewed by the same panel. He made up his mind to shout a defiant ¡Viva La República! in the face of the firing squad.

However, he was taken to the gate of the barracks, and marched with other Republican prisoners to the railway station, and put on a train. They were taken to San Pedro, and imprisoned again. He recalled that he was still in the same uniform, having had no chance to wash or change. Like all his fellow-prisoners, he stank to high heaven. Again the cells had no beds and they slept on bare boards. They had one meal a day — lukewarm water with a few breadcrumbs and beans floating in it. Some of the prisoners who had been there for months had developed scurvy. The prison was run by Spanish military, but above them were the German Gestapo.

Eventually, the British prisoners were loaded onto cattle trucks and dispatched to San Sebastián, and marched through an angry fascist mob to a prison in Ondoretta. A month later, sixty members of the British battalion were taken to the French border and released. They immediately formed into order, and marched into France singing The Internationale. At a local school, they at last stripped off the filthy clothes and were given soap and warm water. After being given fresh clothing, they were taken by rail to Calais. At every station and signal box on the way, there were French railway workers greeting the men with clenched fist salutes.

From Dover they were transported to Victoria Station in London, where a huge crowd of supporters were cheering and singing to welcome the returning heroes. In the crowd were Walter's mother and sister. He was home. Not all volunteers were so lucky. Among the East Midlands volunteers who did not survive the Spanish Civil War were Fred Sykes,

Jack Watson, Roy Watts, Stuart Breedon, Bernard Winfield, Eric Whalley, Fred Turnhill, Robert Grant and Martin Goodman.

The Spanish Civil War ended with the surrender of Madrid in March 1939. Franco and his fascists had triumphed. But another war against the forces of fascism and Nazism would occur six months later, with the beginning of World War Two. Walter, a survivor of the Spanish Civil War, took part in this struggle too, as a member of the British Navy. He was involved in action on the north Russian convoys, and his naval service ended in submarines. He survived WWII too, and after the war worked for the Nottingham Co-op, becoming an active member of the Labour Party and his union USDAW. He died in 1997, at the age of eighty-five.

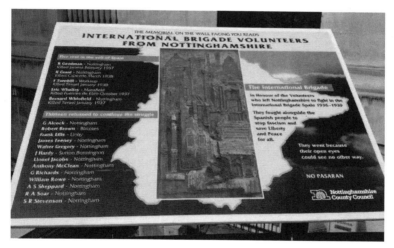

17. Malcolm Pinnegar and the Dirty Thirty

Malcolm "Benny" Pinnegar was the leader of a band of men known as the Dirty Thirty. During the 1984 miners' strike, many mining areas — Yorkshire, Durham, South Wales, Kent, Scotland — had 100% support for the strike, but in Leicestershire, just over thirty of the 2500 miners came out. One who did was Malcolm Pinnegar.

Malcolm was Leicestershire born and bred, growing up in the village of Stoney Stanton. He went to the village school, then to Heathfield High School in Earl Shilton, finishing his schooldays in Burbage. He left school at fifteen, and went into engineering. He worked at Jones & Shipman, then at Bentley Engineering, where machines for the knitting industry were made. He became active in union affairs and was soon the shop steward for the men on the night shift. At Bentley Engineering he learned a lot about wage negotiations, as well as standing up for his colleagues.

Later he moved to Imperial Typewriters, but in the early 1970s he became a coal-miner at Bagworth pit. "One Wednesday in the spring of 1984," he told me, "I came up from working on the afternoon shift to find that Bagworth was being picketed by men from Kent." The Thatcher government was trying to close down a number of Yorkshire pits. Yorkshire miners had gone on strike to defend their jobs, and other areas were supporting them. Kent was a militant area, because many of the men who originally went to work there had been activists who had been blacklisted from their own areas. "At first," Malcolm said with a chuckle, "the Kent miners were the poorest paid in the land, but it wasn't long before they were the best paid."

As Malcolm saw the pickets outside his Bagworth pit, he knew that he would not be going to work the next day. Crossing a picket line was completely against his code, and his way of life. He actually missed a meeting the next day when the Bagworth miners decided to support the strike, but their decision was quickly changed when the Leicestershire NUM officials advised the men not to strike. Most of the men went back to work, apart from Malcolm and a few others.

By Monday, Malcolm had joined the picket line. When it became clear he was one of very few local men to strike, the Kent men persuaded him to go back to work for a week, so that he could try to get his colleagues to come out. Most refused to do so.

In all of Leicestershire's pits only thirty or so men went on strike. The working miners dubbed them the Dirty Thirty, but in a manner that is reminiscent of the soldiers dubbed the Old Contemptibles, the band of strikers took on the label and wore it with pride. Malcolm remembers them all, and their names feature in his reminiscences. The full list of the Dirty Thirty is: Malcolm Pinnegar, Mick Richmond, Mel Elcock, Darren Moore, Dave Douglas, Phil Smith, Cliff and Nigel Jeffery, Bobby and Sammy Girvan, Alan and Mark Findell, Mick Poli, Ron McKillop, Brian Pallet, Mick Barnes, John Chiswell, Andrew Warren, Charlie Burton, Johnny Gamble, Martin Concannon, Barry Draycott, Keith Mellin, John Shirkie, Bob McSporran, Bobby Howard, Gordon Smith, Gordon Birkin, Billy Scott, Dave Bater and Chris Burford. The majority of the thirty (actually thirty-one!) were from Bagworth, three were from Ellistown, and a few were from other pits. "In one mine, only one man joined us," Malcolm recalls, "and that man had some guts."

The Dirty Thirty had a very difficult year. Their working colleagues and some of their neighbours gave them a hard time. Malcolm received anonymous phone calls threatening harm to his family and even threatening his life. One man — a working miner — broke into Malcolm's house one night and threatened to beat him up. Malcolm was not intimidated. He pushed him to the ground and sat on him until the police arrived to arrest the intruder. It was common for the police to take the side of the working miner when there was a dispute between a scab and a striker. However on this occasion, the intruder's mates, waiting outside in the hope that Malcolm would come out of his house, made an error of judgement. They took the handbrake off of the police car and pushed it down the hill. On this occasion the police decided to charge the man who had broken in to beat up the striker.

Malcolm spoke warmly of the support of his wife and daughters, although like many other people he had relatives who were on the other side. Many mining families were split in 1984, with brothers, or fathers and sons, on opposite sides. Malcolm spoke appreciatively of how his wife gave evidence at the case when his intruder was charged. "When the man's lawyer told my wife that she was just saying the same things as me about the event, she just looked him in the eye and said, 'Happen it's the truth then.' She's a very quiet and shy person normally and I was dead proud of her."

Although the vast majority of local miners did not support the Dirty Thirty, Malcolm is very warm in his praise for other Leicestershire people who did. "Hundreds of people helped us raise funds," he says, "and the railwaymen — especially at the Coalville depot — were terrific. Many of them refused to handle coaltrucks, and they, like us, had to live in an area where the consensus was against them." Another local railway depot brought in a large box for railwaymen to bring in tins of food for the striking miners. It was soon full, but one night an anti-strike saboteur took the childish action of ripping the labels off the tins.

One local supporter of the Dirty Thirty recalls how, when collecting tins of food outside an Ashby supermarket under a banner that read BUY AN EXTRA TIN FOR THE STRIKING MINERS' FAMILIES, it was hard to predict the reactions of the public. "One moment someone would tear up our leaflets or even spit at us," he recalled, "and then someone would thrust a £10 note into our hands. When a fierce-looking policewoman came up, we thought she was going to move us on, but she gave us a donation and said she was ashamed of what some officers were doing."

Malcolm was appalled by the behaviour of some police officers, commenting that the local bobbies were not too bad, but those from the Met were the worst. He insisted that he saw a man he knew to be a soldier appear in the police lines in police uniform. One Ashby lady, perfectly respectable and very middle-class, told me that she was arrested while supporting the pickets, taken to a police station and subjected to a humiliating strip search "to teach her a lesson."

Malcolm Pinnegar mentioned to me an occasion when a woman came into the Dirty Thirty's office in Leicester. She explained that her elderly father had just died and left her a few hundred pounds, which she was donating to the cause. The strikers were reluctant to take her money but she insisted, saying that her dad had been in the 1926 General Strike and would want them to have it.

The Dirty Thirty travelled throughout the country, to Italy and even the USA, speaking to audiences about the strike and the reasons for it.

One day Malcolm would be speaking in a Sikh temple, another at a mass meeting at a miners' rally. Wherever he travelled, the mention of the gallant band of men known as the Dirty Thirty brought cheers and applause. He was somewhat surprised in one part of Scotland to have to address two groups of striking miners in the same area, one Catholic the other Protestant. They were both supportive of the Dirty Thirty and generous with their donations but would not meet together in the same hall. They worked at different pits, too, one for each denomination! "That's religion for you," Malcolm said wryly.

There was some humour to be had even during the darkest days. When Malcolm discovered that his phone was being tapped, he took some pleasure in making phone calls with fictitious stories about masses of flying pickets that were coming to a named local pit. Within half an hour he would be laughing as van-loads of police tore off to the peaceful location.

He mentioned with pleasure one Leicester supporter named Tony Stephens, who wrote a play about the Dirty Thirty called *The Sun On Their Backs*. It was performed locally and also in South Wales and in Australia.

The numbers of the Dirty Thirty did vary from time to time. Two working miners from Ellistown pit came out a few months into the strike, saying that their conscience would not let them continue to work while others were on strike. After the strike, Malcolm even discovered an old pit worker who had stayed at home for the full period of the strike, unknown to the other striking miners. "Did the number go down as well as up?" I asked him innocently. "It did not," Malcolm retorted. "Not one member of the Dirty Thirty went back until the end."

The strike ended in defeat for the strikers in March 1985. "I saw many grown men, big tough miners, crying on that day," Malcolm told me. "It was not easy for us to go back down Bagworth pit with men who regarded us as the enemy. Actually, we were lucky at Bagworth, because the manager and one of his deputies were very fair and stamped down on any intimidation." He says that the atmosphere at Bagworth may have been unpleasant, but that it was a nightmare at the other Leicestershire pits. The members of the Dirty Thirty in those pits were real heroes, he believes.

After the defeat, most of Britain's mines were closed down, reducing their number from 170 to twelve, then to zero. When Bagworth closed, Malcolm went to work in a mine at Keresley, near Coventry, until that was closed too in 1992. Malcolm, whose fundraising skills had been honed to perfection during the strike, went to work for Leicester City Football Club on their lottery scheme. In later years he worked as a lorry driver.

Malcolm did not regard himself as a hero. "There were thirty heroes," he told me, "plus all the men and women who supported us at great risk to themselves. Some lost their jobs, and were blacklisted, and some had to put up with threats and intimidation."

Throughout his life, Malcolm took pride in his role of leading the Dirty Thirty. "I know what we did was right," he said, "and the working miners now know what we did was right. Some have even come up to me over the years and said so. My conscience is clear and I think that history will prove that the stand we took was the right one."

Alun Parry, a Liverpudlian singer-songwriter, wrote a magnificent song about the Dirty Thirty and Malcolm's part within it:

> Let me tell you a story
> For I really can't ignore
> The happenings in Leicestershire
> In 1984
> Two thousand and five hundred
> Walked across that picket line
> But a tiny band of miners
> Would not go into the mine
>
> They were called the Dirty Thirty
> So they wore that name with pride
> As the only striking miners
> They stood against the tide
> And if you call them heroes
> They would surely disagree
> But the Dirty Thirty and their kin
> Are all heroes to me
>
> The railwaymen at Coalville
> They backed the miners too

And when a coal train came along
They would not let it through
And the women they were mighty
Maybe mightier than the men
They suffered so much hardship
But they'd do it all again

So here's to Malcolm Pinnegar
Or "Benny" to his friends
Who led the Dirty Thirty
Till the strike came to an end
And here's to all the other lads
So principled and true
And those who stood beside them
As a worker's meant to do

They were called the Dirty Thirty
So they wore that name with pride
As the only striking miners
They stood against the tide
And if you call them heroes
They would surely disagree
But the Dirty Thirty and their kin
Are all heroes to me

Two Leicestershire film-makers, Brian Langtry and Dr Len Holden, made a documentary about the Dirty Thirty, featuring Malcolm, and his co-leader Mick "Richo" Richmond.

Malcolm died on 6th April 2012, after being diagnosed with pancreatic cancer in 2010. I attended his funeral at Nuneaton Crematorium, and it finished with a wonderful statement of his views and outlook, read out by his grandson. After reading it out, he said, "My granddad wrote this out for me shortly before he died." The Dirty Thirty member sitting next to me smiled and said, "Good old Benny. Still having the last word!"

A true epitaph to a working-class hero.

18. Jeremiah Brandreth and the Pentrich Rising

The Pentrich Rising took place in Derbyshire in 1817. The first two decades of the nineteenth century were a turbulent time. Conditions were hard and working people and their families were suffering great hardship. The war with France had ended and soldiers were returning, adding to the unemployment and poverty that were already there. In 1815 the Corn Law was brought back to keep bread prices from falling, and in 1816 there had been a disastrous harvest. In Derbyshire there was snow in early June and no grass grew until the end of that month. People could no longer afford to buy bread or potatoes. Hunger was everywhere and anger was widespread.

The government was in a state of panic. There had been two revolutions — one in France and a second in America — and conditions in England were ripe for a third. When the East Midlands became the centre of machine-breaking — the workers rightly blamed the introduction of stocking and lacemaking machines for their poverty — the government responded by making the breaking of machinery a specific hanging offence, along with the burning of hayricks, another revolutionary activity.

Derby-born writer Edward Garner states, "The ending of the war years saw a growing polarisation of society. Class differences were becoming more defined, adding to the government's growing unease." Clarence Daniel of Eyam, in his book *A Peakland Portfolio*, writes: "The Derbyshire Rising was a short chapter in the long story of the class struggle in which the working man has repeatedly pressed his claim for fairer wages and better living conditions. It was a revolt against hunger, poverty and unemployment. It was a protest against the tyranny, inhumanity and misrule of a government entirely out of sympathy with the labouring classes."

Some of the pressure for reform was channelled through political debating societies. Organisations known as Hampden Clubs sprang up all over the country, set up to discuss and to petition Parliament for social and political reform. Tom Paine's influential book *The Rights of Man*, published in 1791, was widely quoted. Radical Members of Parliament like Lord Byron and Derbyshire's Sir Francis Burdett argued the case for social change, but the government continued to see all change as dangerous and all reformers as revolutionaries.

And there were those who believed that only direct action and armed rebellion would achieve the long-awaited change. One such was thirty-one year old Jeremiah Brandreth, an unemployed local framework knitter and former soldier. Jeremiah, from Sutton-in-Ashfield, had formerly served with the 28th Foot, a prominent infantry regiment in Wellington's army. Moreover he could read and write. He really was the government's worst fear — an educated radical, with military experience.

Jeremiah Brandreth was born in London in 1785, but the following year his family moved to Barnstaple in Devon. He received a good education there. After his time as a soldier, he moved to Nottinghamshire. The date is not known, but it was some years before his marriage to Ann Bridget in Sutton-in Ashfield in 1811.

Because of his military background he was nicknamed the Nottingham Captain, He had a striking appearance — "with very black whiskers" — and a charismatic personality. He was the leader of the men of Pentrich who met to plan an armed rising against the hated government. The Derbyshire rebellion was, they believed, to be just one part of a national revolution that would march on London and create a new government with Sir Francis Burdett of Foremark Hall in south Derbyshire as its prime minister. They had even designed a new flag, a red, white and green tricolour.

On Sunday 8 June 1817, Jeremiah walked seventeen miles from Sutton to Pentrich to attend a meeting, held in the White Horse Inn in Pentrich, where the landlady, Ann Weightman, was the mother of one of the rebels. Jeremiah Brandreth pointed to the map on the table and indicated the route the men would need to take to march first to Nottingham and then on to London. He showed where they would meet up with other parties of men with the same aim. They were to meet contingents from South Wingfield, Alfreton and Crich the next night at Hunt's Barn, then march to Butterley, where they would be reinforced by men from Sheffield and Chesterfield, and seize the local ironworks. Some of the men had grievances with a local magistrate, Colonel Halton, and others with Mr Jessop, the owner of the Butterley ironworks. It was agreed that these two men would have to be shot. The Pentrich men would then be joined by men from Codnor and Heanor, march to Nottingham Forest and then with the help of rebels from Nottingham they would seize that city.

Two of the men present were William Turner and Charles Swaine, who, like Jeremiah, were former soldiers. One of the government's fears was that soldiers returning from the Napoleonic wars would make common cause with the working-class poor, and bring their military expertise with them. Turner was the quartermaster, and he told the meeting that hidden in a quarry in Wingfield were forty pikes. Guns would be coming from both Wingfield and Ripley. They also had one barrel of gunpowder and a quantity of lead for making bullets. When asked what would happen when they ran out of lead, he said that there was plenty of lead on church roofs along their route.

Jeremiah got everyone present to sing a rousing anthem that he had written:

> Everyone his skill must try
> He must turn out and not deny
> No bloody soldier must he dread
> He must turn out and fight for bread
> The time is come, you plainly see
> The government opposed must be.

One of the most enthusiastic of the revolutionaries at the meeting was a man known only as Oliver. He was the one who laughed at any of the men who expressed doubts. He was the one who encouraged Brandreth and Turner to put their plans into immediate action. Oliver was of genteel appearance, with a good speaking voice, standing erect at six feet tall, with light-coloured hair and red whiskers. He wore a fashionable brown coat over a black waistcoat, dark blue pantaloons and black wellington-style boots. He seemed a worthy recruit to the cause, and everyone at the meeting trusted him.

One of the leaders of the Pentrich group was absent from the meeting at the White Horse. He was Ann Weightman's brother, sixty-four-year-old Thomas Bacon, a keen reader of Thomas Paine, a self-educated and well-travelled man who had even visited America. Bacon had been a frameworker, and it is therefore highly likely that he had been involved in the Luddite movement, as had Jeremiah. He had also worked at the local Butterley ironworks. He had been involved in the setting up of a number of Hampden Clubs, including the one at Ripley.

The next day, Monday 9 June, a number of men made their way to Hunt's Barn in South Wingfield, among them Jeremiah Brandreth and George Weightman. Among the volunteers from the South Wingfield area were farmers Samuel and Daniel Hunt. Another was James Shipman, who asked about the provision of food for the march, Jeremiah confidently assuring him that every man would receive bread, beef and rum. Asked about what would happen to their families, the ebullient leader said that once a provisional government had been formed their wives and children would receive all the food they needed.

At the barn, pikes, a few guns and a little ammunition were distributed. The number of men was probably less than sixty at this time, and the number was constantly changing as more volunteers joined. It was not all one way: one farmer named Tomlinson deserted after the Hunt's Barn meeting and another rebel, Elijah Hall, also left the group.

Will Turner and Charlie Swaine marshalled the company, placing the men with guns at the front of a double file, and those with pikes at the rear. The little army, still numbering less than a hundred, marched to Butterley ironworks to try to recruit the six hundred and fifty men who were employed there. The manager, Mr Goodwin, refused to let Brandreth address his employees and warned the rebels that their enterprise would end upon the gallows. Surprisingly, Brandreth marched his men away without a shot being fired. It seems likely that he was keen to proceed with the march south, and could not spare the time to take the ironworks by force.

As the men marched off, a young recruit rode up to the ironworks with a bag full of lead bullets, badly needed by the band of revolutionaries. Goodwin dragged the man off his horse and took the ammunition from him. Even at this early stage, things were not going well for the rebels. Not only had the expected recruits from Chesterfield and Sheffield failed to appear, the weather had now turned to heavy rain.

The rather damp volunteers marched on to Ripley, where they were delighted at the sight of considerable reinforcements from Belper and Heage. In better spirits, the little Derbyshire army moved on to Codnor, where they took shelter in three public houses — the Glass House, the French Horn and the New Inn — while Will Turner and Sam Hunt went into the town to seek further recruits. Their mission proved successful and they returned with forty or fifty local men, then a further party of seventy arrived from Swanwick. Things were looking up. The army now numbered between two and three hundred.

At Langley Mill, they met up with George Weightman who had been sent ahead to ascertain what was happening in Nottingham. His information was not encouraging; there had been very few rebels in Nottingham and these had easily been subdued by the military. However, Weightman addressed the men, giving them a more encouraging report than the facts justified. The rebel army reached the racecourse at Nottingham Forest, and after an encounter with the armed caretaker, the Derbyshire men continued towards Nottingham.

At Eastwood, a magistrate saw the advancing rebels and informed the military authorities. A party of the 15th Hussars marched out from Nottingham and, at 6am, they met the rebels at Giltbrook. Jeremiah Brandreth formed his men up into a defensive line, but as the Hussars prepared to charge, many of the rebels broke ranks and fled. The remaining men, including Brandreth, stood firm but were soon routed. Forty men were taken there and then, and many more were arrested within a few days.

One of the first leaders taken was Will Turner, a forty-six-year-old stonemason from South Wingfield, who had seen sixteen years service as a soldier. Isaac Ludlam, hunted down near Uttoxeter, was a fifty-two-year-old quarry owner and a noted Methodist preacher. George Weightman, a young sawyer whose widowed mother kept the White Horse Inn at Pentrich, was arrested near Sheffield. Jeremiah Brandreth managed to get to Bristol where he tried unsuccessfully to board a ship to America; eventually he returned to his wife and children in Sutton-in-Ashfield, where he was soon taken into custody.

Thirty-six of the rebels were charged with high treason. At their trial in Derby, the prosecution was led by the Attorney General, Sir Samuel Shepherd, and the presiding judge was Sir Richard Richards. The jury of twelve local landowners knew what was expected of them and brought in the verdict required. Three men — Brandreth, Ludlam and Turner — were sentenced to death by hanging and posthumous beheading. Eleven others, including Thomas Bacon and George Weightman, were sentenced to transportation for life, and three more for fourteen years. A further six men were gaoled for periods between six months and two years. No evidence was produced in the case of the remaining twelve men, and these were freed.

Jeremiah Brandreth, Isaac Ludlam and William Turner were executed in Derby on Friday 7 November, outside the county gaol. On that day the three condemned men had their final communion in the prison chapel, and Jeremiah wrote a letter to his pregnant wife, Ann. They were taken to the scaffold on a hurdle, and then were publicly hanged before a crowd of Derby people.

Brandreth ascended the platform first, and addressed the crowd with the words "God be with you all, all but Lord Castlereagh!" There are those who claim his words were "God be with you all, and Lord

Castlereagh", but this seems unlikely, given that Castlereagh was the most hated of the government ministers, and the most opposed to any kind of reform. Indeed, the poet Shelley wrote of him, "I met murder on the way, He had a mask like Castlereagh." Ludlam's final words were uncontroversial, but Will Turner proclaimed bitterly, "This is the work of the government and Oliver."

The three men were hanged from three nooses at 12.30pm, watched by a crowd that included those men awaiting transportation, who were marched out in chains to see their comrades die. Half an hour later, the bodies of the three men were hauled into a kneeling position and the platform covered with sawdust. One by one the necks of the three dead men were placed on the block.

Jeremiah's head was the first to be severed, though the axeman failed to sever it cleanly and the gruesome task had to be completed by an assistant using a knife. The executioner held the bloody head aloft by its hair and proclaimed, "Behold the head of a traitor, Jeremiah Brandreth."

A contemporary drawing of the execution of Jeremiah Brandreth.

By now the crowd were groaning and booing, rather than cheering as they were meant to do. The soldiers present feared a civil disturbance, and drew their swords. However, despite having to watch the same indignities committed on the bodies of Ludlam and Turner, the ceremony passed off without further trouble.

But why had William Turner referred to the government and Oliver? He was talking about the man who had seemed to be such a keen supporter of the Pentrich rising. It soon became apparent that Oliver was not all he seemed. He had been present among the Derbyshire revolutionaries because he was being paid by the government to be there. His real name was William Oliver, though he was also known under the name William Richards. He had been in prison for debt and for bigamy, but these crimes had been wiped out when he became a government agent, working for the Home Office. With the information he was sending back to his paymasters, the Derbyshire revolt could easily have been nipped in the bud at an early stage, but for its own reasons the government decided to let it go on. They needed it to happen in order to put it down very publicly and very savagely.

Before the trial took place, the editor of the *Leeds Mercury*, Edward Baines, published an article, naming Oliver as a spy in government pay. Baines claimed that not only was Oliver a spy, he was also a driving force behind the rising, suggesting to the Derbyshire men that they take up arms. Oliver was a classic agent provocateur. A furious Sir Francis Burdett, the reform-minded MP from south Derbyshire, demanded to know why Oliver the spy had spread the tale that Burdett was to be the Prime Minister after the successful revolution. Had the government instructed their agent to misuse his name? Lord Liverpool conceded that Oliver was indeed their agent, but denied telling him to name Sir Francis. Saying that all governments had used spies and would always do so, Lord Liverpool said that on occasions such men would "from zeal in their business" go too far.

During the trial, the legend "REMEMBER OLIVER THE SPY" appeared on walls throughout Derby, in an attempt to remind the judge and jury of Oliver's part in the insurrection, but — unfortunately for the men on trial — Oliver never appeared in court. After the trial and execution, Oliver, now an embarrassment to his employers, was sent to South Africa, where he lived under the name William Oliver Jones. There he was given a sinecure, becoming the Inspector of Buildings in Cape Colony.

One further mystery remains, and that concerns Thomas Bacon. Despite not being physically present during the rebellion, Bacon was known to be a leader of the Pentrich men. He was not sentenced to death. Some historians have deduced from this that he too may have been in government pay. To me this seems extremely unlikely. Thomas Bacon had spent his whole life agitating for social reform, supporting the French and American revolutions, and spreading the ideas of Thomas Paine. I do not see a man of his beliefs and principles selling out to the corrupt government of his time. And although he escaped the death penalty, Thomas Bacon and his brother were transported for life. What is possible is that to convict Bacon of being a leader of the insurrectionists, Oliver the spy would have had to give evidence in court. That was something the government was very keen to avoid.

It is sometimes claimed the poet Percy Bysshe Shelley was present in Derby at the execution of Brandreth, Ludlam and Turner. There seems little factual evidence for this, though Shelley did write a political pamphlet entitled *We Pity the Plumage But Forget the Dying Bird*. In it, the poet contrasts the public mourning that followed the death of Princess Charlotte, daughter of the Prince Regent, with the apathy that followed the deaths of the leaders of the Derbyshire rising, whom he saw as victims of political intrigue. "Fetters heavier than iron weigh upon us, because they bind our souls," he wrote. "Let us follow the corpse of British liberty slowly and reverentially to its tomb, and if some glorious phantom should appear... let us say that the spirit of Liberty has risen from its grave."

Jeremiah Brandreth believed, or was persuaded by Oliver the spy, that the Pentrich rising was one part of a mass rising that was occurring all over the nation. Indeed, he must have thought that the revolution was international since he told his followers at the Hunt's Barn meeting that the next day at 10am a rising would take place in England, France and Ireland. Apart from a minor disturbance in Huddersfield, easily put down, it was only in Derbyshire that men actually took arms and rose against the corruption of their government. The Pentrich Rising was England's last revolution, but it was doomed to fail. Thanks to Oliver the spy, Lord Sidmouth, the Home Secretary, had known of the intended rebellion for many weeks before it happened. He even knew the date it was to occur; he could have stopped it, but chose to let it happen and be suppressed.

After the rising, the authorities continued to take action against those who might have supported the rebels. The village of Pentrich stood on land belonging to the Duke of Devonshire, and after the trial the Duke had many of its houses pulled down and their inhabitants turned out. Twenty of the 122 houses were demolished and the population of Pentrich was reduced from 726 to 508. It was no doubt hoped that pulling down the houses would also mean that memory of the rebels would also be wiped out.

The bodies of the three executed men were buried in an unmarked common grave in the churchyard of St Werburgh's in Derby. Although no monument to them exists, they are still remembered as part of Derbyshire working-class history in both song and story. *The Liberty Tree*, a play based on the event, was performed in Derby in 1980. Singer-songwriters John Young and Keith Jones have written a number of songs about the Derbyshire men who took part in the Pentrich Rising, one of which concludes: "The fire that Brandreth kindled, today still burns as bright/That working men should organise and fight to get their rights." And on the 200th anniversary of the uprising, commemorative events took place in Derbyshire and Nottingham, and several pamphlets and books were printed.

Perhaps the attempt to annihilate the memory of those who took part in England's last revolution was less successful than the authorities hoped!

Bibliography

Books:

Invergordon Mutineer by Len Wincott (Weidenfield & Nicolson, 1974)

George Fox & the Valiant Sixty by Elfrida Vipont (Hamish Hamilton, 1973)

The Weaker Vessel: Woman's Lot in Seventeenth Century England by Antonia Fraser (Heinemann, 1984)

Shifting Horizons by Lynn Beaton (Canary Press, 1985)

A People's History of Leicester by Ned Newitt (Breedon Books, 2008)

Victorian Leicester by Malcolm Elliott (Amberley Publishing, 2010)

The Shallow Grave by Walter Gregory (Victor Gollancz Ltd, 1986, Five Leaves, 1996/2019)

The Hard Way Up by Hannah Mitchell (ed Geoffrey Mitchell) (Virago, 1977)

Bows Against the Barons by Geoffrey Trease (Martin Lawrence, 1934, Lawrence & Wishart, 1948)

Friends of Alice Wheeldon by Sheila Rowbotham (Pluto Press, 1986)

The Plot to Kill Lloyd George by Nicola Rippon (Wharncliffe Books, 2009)

Free But Not Easy by Bas Barker & Lynda Straker (Derbyshire County Council, 1989)

Bravery and Deception: the Pentrich Revolt of 1817 by Julian Atkinson (Nottinghamshire & Derbyshire Labour History Society, 2016)

1817 A Recipe For Revolution: Reflections on the Pentrich Rising by Michael Parkin (2014)

The Life of Jeremiah Brandreth by John Dring (Pentrich & South Wingfield Revolution Group, 2015)

The Dirty Thirty by David Bell (Five Leaves, 2009)

Articles:

"A Friend of Liberty" by Dr Alan Doring (*The Nottingham Historian*, 64)

"Loyalism in Newark" by Dr Alan Doring (*The Nottingham Historian*, 71)

Online:

"The Volunteers" by Richard Baxell
(www.richardbaxell.info/volunteers)

"The Who's Who of Radical Leicester" by Ned Newitt
(nednewitt.com/whoswho)